Swissair Down

A Pilot's View of the Crash at Peggys Cove

Don Ledger

NIMBUS
PUBLISHING

Nimbus Publishing Limited
PO Box 9301, Station A
Halifax, Nova Scotia B3K 5N5
(902) 455-4286

Design: Terri Strickland
Printed and bound in Canada.

Canadian Cataloguing in Publication Data
Ledger, Don, 1945-
Swissair down
ISBN 1-55109-301-4
Aircraft accidents—Investigation—Nova Scotia. 2. Swissair. I. Title.
2. TL553.5.L42 2000 363.12'46509716 C00-950062-6

Canadä

Nimbus Publishing acknowledges the support of the Canada Council and the Department of Canadian Heritage.

Contents

Acknowledgements

I would like to thank the following people for their help and support: retired Air Traffic Controller and pilot Doug Betts for his expertise; pilot Kevin Layden for his Coast Guard insights; pilot Phil Chatterton for his expertise on Kapton Wiring; pilot Larry Vance, of the Canadian Transportation Safety Board, for his unreserved answers; Chief Petty Officer Glenn Adams for spending a day with me to share his world of the Canadian Navy Clearance Diver; pilot Grant Kennedy for his forbearance and for the flight; pilot-in-training Mike Doiron, of Transportation Canada, for pointing me in the right direction at the beginning; Pastor Phil Williams for talking to me about a painful subject; David and Hazel Hirtle, and Harris and Audrey Backman, for their testimony; fisherman Granville Cleveland for sharing his story; pilot Brian Chappell for letting me bend his ear; and Natacha Pressacco at the Consulat général de Suisse for her help. Reporters at The Chronicle Herald and The Daily News were a great source of preliminary information, as were the CBC and ATV news. And perhaps no medium but the Internet could have provided me with as much information as I was able to discover there. Finally, I want to thank Dorothy Blythe, my publisher at Nimbus who took the time to question the manuscript and to see that I got it right.

Preface

About three hundred people, many of them pilots, were attending the Fly-In at Stanley Airfield in 1995. I heard the aircraft taking off and turned from a display table full of aircraft pictures and models to confirm my suspicion that this was a Lake Amphibian about to take off from Runway 27. The prop makes a very distinct sound. Since I've always had a soft spot for float planes and Amphibians, I experienced something akin to a Pavlovian response. I had to turn and watch.

Many people at the field watched with interest, as most will when a plane takes off. The aircraft laboured down the runway and well past the usual point of rotation. For the untrained observer this was not a concern, but to me and the other pilots watching, particularly those familiar with this field, we knew something was not right.

The airplane, now quite far down the 2,400-ft runway, lumbered into the thin, warm air. The windsock was hanging limp so there would be no help from a headwind to shorten the takeoff run, making the aircraft think it was going faster than it really was, providing additional and "free" lift. We pilots breathed a short-lived sigh of relief.

The LA-4 Lake Amphibian, engine at full throttle, settled back on the runway, then bounced slowly once more into the air. The Amphibian was now fully two-thirds down the runway and still struggling to get aloft. It sagged again but stayed airborne. The plane was making its way toward 15-m (50 ft) treetops just west of the end of Runway 27.

The LA-4 finally got about 12 m (40 ft) in altitude. Though the nose of the airplane was inclined slightly upward, the machine did not seem to be gaining altitude. I watched in helpless desperation, while the Lake Amphibian laboured just above stall speed, through that hot, humid summer air.

For a moment it appeared the Amphibian was safe, slightly higher than the trees, until it sagged and ploughed into the treetops. The prop was still clear of the leaves and branches, so it continued to push the airplane as vegetation slipped along the hull and caressed the bottoms of the wings. The Lake Amphibian was fighting a losing battle. As friction dragged the airspeed to the point of wing stall, the left wing struck a treetop. Three metres of the left wing tore loose, stealing the life-giving lift it had been producing. The plane promptly stalled. With the right wing still generating lift, the aircraft rolled to the left through 180 degrees, then completely inverted. The machine dove into the ground 12 m (40 ft) below, its propeller still generating thrust. It impacted at about 80 degrees to the vertical, killing the two pilots instantly and critically injuring the occupant of the back seat.

I didn't see the impact, but I'll never forget the surprising sound of that airplane hitting the forest floor. It was like someone had dropped a huge metal box from a great height—*bang* and *crunch*. When we reached the site of the impact, and extricated the sole survivor from the fuel-soaked crumpled mass, a fellow pilot told me that one of the pilots who had been killed was a friend of mine. I had met him only a year earlier and I liked him right away. A tall, quiet, affable man in his mid-thirties, he made his living crop-dusting and entertaining people in an aerobatic airplane. He was a pilot experienced in navigating a heavily-loaded plane at low levels and making tight turns.

An LA-4 Lake Amphibian, similar to the aircraft that crashed at Stanley Airfield on September 3, 1995, killing two of the three aboard.

Later, we learned that the aircraft was over its designed weight limits (over gross), and that the piston rings in a couple of the cylinders of the four-cylinder engine were cracked. As a result it wasn't developing its full rating of 180 hp. And we were all aware that there was little lift in the air. Surprisingly, this pilot had chosen a shorter runway.

I returned to the airfield later, numbed by what I had seen and by the death of a friend. I was tired, too, from our successful attempt at getting a fire hose to the crash site, several hundred metres from the nearest road, and from helping to transport the critically-injured passenger through dense brush to a power line right-of-way for the paramedics. Fortunately, there were two doctors on the field at the time of the crash, and they helped stabilize the passenger, though their prognosis was that he would not make it.

Almost immediately there was a call from the media. Since I was the Fly-In chairman and used to dealing with press in my day job, I handled the calls. They were unremitting. One call was clearly from a relative seeking information. I pleaded ignorance and gave them, as instructed, the number of the Windsor RCMP. For some three days I fielded questions and provided details for the media.

That incident occurred more than four years ago. The critically-injured passenger, the son of the owner of the aircraft, completely recovered. He is now an avid flyer and owns an airplane. (He remembers nothing of what happened four hours before the crash.)

I, too, still fly, a little older and a little wiser. And, like those people who participated in the search for Flight 111—although my experience pales at the magnitude of the Swissair disaster—I'll never forget my experience that day.

A note about the content: Any author writing about aviation becomes acutely aware of the overwhelming technology involved. As a pilot, I expected it. There are technical terms in this book, which I endeavour to explain in the body of the text or in the glossary at the back.

Canadian readers, resigned as they are to the metric system, may be surprised to discover that aviation abounds with Imperial measurements. The United States is the largest producer of aircraft in the world, so their use of terms and measurements prevail. Aviation also embraces nautical terms such as nautical units and knots. To further complicate matters, the American gallon is one-fifth smaller than the Imperial gallon but is used extensively to compute the fuel on any American-built aircraft, because that is the unit used in the operational handbook for the aircraft. For Canadian readers, these Imperial measurements are converted, in many cases, to their metric equivalents; however, in quotations or dialogue that use the standard lingo of aviation, there is no conversion so as not to hinder the narrative flow. Following the glossary, I have included a set of conversion tables for those not conversant with the nautical system of measurement.

Another difficulty in writing about the Swissair tragedy was maintaining the chronology of the disaster. From the outset, it was necessary to explain a particular aspect concerning the crash or the investigation in a related chapter at the risk of interfering with the flow of the actual or "real time" of the event being discussed. This necessitated short digressions, rather than endless footnotes.

Swissair Down covers more than a year, and even at the time of writing, the Transportation Safety Board's investigation is ongoing. Drawing from the available evidence, research, interviews with various parties involved in the Swissair tragedy, and my own knowledge and experience of aviation, I offer theories as to why Flight 111 crashed, theories that I think will be borne out by the passage of time.

Swissair MD-11
Profile and Specifications

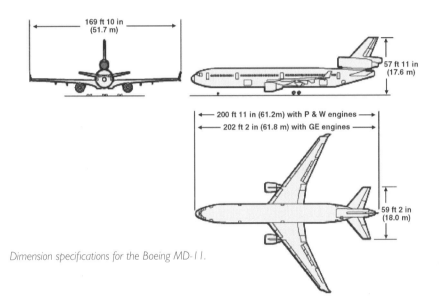

Dimension specifications for the Boeing MD-11.

A Swissair Boeing MD-11 in flight, a sister ship to Flight -111.

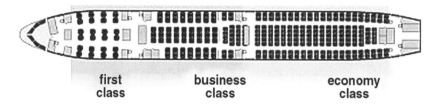

first
class

business
class

economy
class

Seat locations, passenger version, on Boeing MD-11

The flight deck and working space for the pilot and co-pilot on a Boeing MD-11.

Swissair Flight 111 MD-11 — Aircraft General Information

Manufacturer	McDonnell Douglas
Type and Model	MD-11A
Registration	HB-IWF
Year of Manufacture	1991
Serial Number	48448
Certificate of Airworthiness	Yes
Total Airframe Time/Number of Cycles	36,041 hrs / 6560
Engine Type (number of)	Pratt & Whitney 4462 (3)
Maximum Allowable Take-off Mass	285,990 kg
Recommended Fuel Type(s)	Jet A, Jet A1, JP5, JP8, Jet B, JP4
Fuel Type Used	Jet A

CHAPTER ONE

From New York to
Peggys Cove

If you stand, as I have, in a big open airfield—miles from any town or city—and stare straight up into the canopy of stars on a clear night, you can watch the airliners of the world passing overhead, five to seven miles closer to the Milky Way than you are. You rarely hear them, but you can trace their paths across the sky. Their wing-tip strobes and flashing tail- and belly lights announce their presence to the ground observer and to other wide-bodied jets sharing that same aerial corridor, separated from one another by prescribed lateral distances and vertical space dictated by little lines traced on air traffic controllers' radar screens.

Each light tracing its way across that starry blanket signifies the in- dividual hopes and dreams of a collective body of people sharing in the ad- venture of flight across the Atlantic Ocean. Every once in a while, one of those little lights falls like a meteor, but with a more precious center than any meteor can hold. As always, the mighty Atlantic waits dispassion- ately, claiming whatever dares to cross that suddenly finds itself in dis- tress. It makes no judgements and gives no quarter. The night of September 2, 1998, was one of those times.

At 9:58:15.8 P.M. local time, ("15.8" indicates 15-and-8-tenths of a sec- ond) Swissair Flight 111—flying out of John F. Kennedy (JFK) Airport in New York, on a flight path for Geneva, Switzerland—made first contact with Air Traffic Control (ATC) at Moncton Center. During the next thirty- four minutes, communications would culminate in one of the worst air disasters in commercial aviation history and the worst in Canadian avia- tion history, resulting in the death of all 229 passengers and crew aboard the MD-11 tri-jet. This would instigate the most extensive investigation into the crash of an airliner in the history of modern air disasters.

Captain Urs Zimmermann, the pilot of Swissair Flight 111.

Stefan Loëw, the co-pilot on Swissair Flight 111.

It began as a routine flight. The forty-nine-year-old pilot of Swissair Flight 111, Capt. Urs Zimmermann, received his takeoff clearances from ATC at JFK Airport and taxied to position on Runway 13 Right (R13). After holding for a few moments, he advanced the three throttles of the Swissair-registered aircraft, tail number HB-IWF, a McDonnell Douglas MD-11. With First Officer Stephan Loëw's left hand clamped over Zimmerman's right—a precautionary measure to ensure that if the pilot were suddenly incapacitated the aircraft would not be put off the end of the runway because the throttles had been retarded inadvertently— Zimmermann guided the aircraft straight down R13, JFK's longest runway.

The MD-11's speed advanced to V1 (velocity one) the go, no-go point. At a speed of 139 knots, Captain Zimmermann pulled back gently on the control column, rotating the aircraft to a nose up position, lifted off at V2, the velocity required to lift the plane off the ground, and was airborne by 8:18 P.M., New York time.

The Swissair tri-jet climbed steadily into the night sky, heading a bit southward before coming around to an assigned heading of 81 degrees magnetic— the heading that would eventually take it northeastward, up the Atlantic coast toward Eastern Canada, and along one of the busiest air corridors in the world. In fact, Swissair Flight 111 was inserted

into a steady stream of about five hundred aircraft that would fly this corridor most of the night.

Both pilots were Swiss citizens and MD-11 instructors with a considerable amount of flying time between them. With twenty-seven years in-
vested in Swissair as a pilot, eleven of them as a captain, Zimmermann
had over nine thousand hours to his credit, nine hundred of them as a
pilot on the MD-11. He was a likely candidate for his additional duties as
a check pilot for Swissair, meaning he checked out other pilots' flying pro-
ficiency on Swissair's aircraft, particularly when pilot's were upgrading
to a heavier and perhaps more complex airplane. That coming Friday,
Captain Zimmermann's family was going to hold a birthday party at home
with his wife and three children in honour of his fiftieth birthday.

Thirty-six-year-old Stephan Loëw was also married and the father of
three children. He had twenty-eight hundred hours as a pilot, two hundred twenty of which he had earned flying as co-pilot on Swissair's MD-
11s. Like his captain, he was eager to get home. There was work ahead
because he and his family were in the process of moving into a new house.

Flight 111 climbed without incident to its assigned altitude of 33,000
ft en route to Geneva, Switzerland, anticipating an arrival time of 9:30
A.M. Swiss local daylight saving time. The trip would have taken about
seven hours in total, with the MD-11 touching down in Zurich at approximately 3:30 A.M.., New York time. (New York is in the Eastern Time
Zone, whereas Nova Scotia is one hour ahead in the Atlantic Time Zone
and five hours behind Zurich time.)

The Boeing MD-11 tri-jet was originally built by McDonnell Douglas
and now by Boeing, who acquired McDonnell Douglas' assets in a recent
merger. The MD-11 is an upgrade of the earlier model DC-10. It is almost
6 m (19 ft) longer than the DC-10 and capable of carrying about fifty more
passengers. It can be fitted with three different types of jet engines manufactured by three giants in the power plant business: Pratt & Whitney,
General Electric, and Rolls Royce. The latter is likely to power aircraft
used in the United Kingdom and other European countries; however, in
this case Flight 111 was fitted with three Pratt & Whitney PW 4460 tur-
bofan jets, each capable of producing 60,000 lbs of thrust. On the MD-11
tri-jet there is one engine mounted close inboard on each wing, and a
third (engine no. 2) mounted on the tail where the vertical stabilizer and
rudder assembly meets the empennage, or rear section of the fuselage.

The MD-11, no longer built, found favour with Swissair but few other

companies. The tri-jet was likely chosen by Swissair as a compromise between two engines and four engines for overseas work. Many commercial airline pilots in the late 1980s and the early 1990s were not fond of flying over large bodies of water like the Atlantic Ocean in a passenger liner
with only two jet engines. In the tri-jet configuration, if one engine were
to fail, there would be two more to run on. It added a safety net, but had
an advantage over the four-engine jets, which are gas-guzzlers and need-
lessly lug that extra engine, creating drag on the wing. However, after several crashes with the forerunner DC-10—compressor vanes in that rear
engine failed, cutting through the hydraulic lines in the rear—they began
to lose favour, even with pilots. Nowadays, highly reliable twin-engine
wide-bodied jets ply the Atlantic and Pacific routes in the thousands, and
the MD-11s have been pretty much relegated to a few oriental airlines,
and Swissair, with the major numbers hauling cargo for Federal Express
in the United States.

At 61.6 m (202 ft, 2 in.) in length and with a wingspan of 51.7 m (169
ft, 10 in.), the MD-11 is a large aircraft with three passenger class con-
figurations: 24 in first class, 57 in business class, and 204 in economy
class, for a total of 285 passengers. All classes have two aisles which begin
behind the cockpit and continue straight through to the after cabin. The
MD-11 has a fuel capacity of 27,047 L (7,145 US gallons), which gives it
an optimum range of 13,239 km (8,228 statute miles). This tremendous
fuel capacity would create a problem for the crew of Flight 111 forty minutes into the flight, possibly leading to a decision that resulted in the death
of everyone on board.

On September 2, Flight 111 was fully loaded with fuel, luggage, cargo,
215 passengers and 14 crew. The cargo weighed over 13,000 kg (30,000
lbs) and consisted of mail, a rare Picasso painting, millions of dollars in diamonds and jewellery and American currency bound for Swiss banks.

It had recently recorded its six thousandth flight since its maiden
flight on August 5, 1991, and had recycled over twelve thousand times,
meaning that the airplane had an equal number of takeoffs and landings.
Until the evening of September 2. It had recently recorded over thirty-
five thousand hours of airborne time on its airframe.

In the cockpit, Captain Zimmermann and First Officer Loëw were
taking care of business. Like all modern airliners, the MD-11 lacks the
myriad switches and dials that were the signatures of all airline cockpits
until the early 1980s. Since the early 1990s, the instrument panel in all
of MD-11s is dominated by six 20.5-cm (8-in.) Cathode Ray Tube (CRT)

screens, which electronically display the faces of the older mechanical instruments (a.k.a. steam gauges) that used to be separately mounted on the instrument panel. Designed by McDonnell Douglas and Honeywell's Air Transport Systems Division, the CRTs are strung across the panel. The two outer screens, one in front of each pilot, make up the Primary Flight Display (PFD).

On one side of this screen is a vertical indicator of the aircraft's speed in knots, while the other side displays the altitude. The central image on the PFD screen is the Attitude Indicator (AI), which tells the pilots which attitude the airplane is in—climbing, diving, banking, or a combination. There is also an arc at the bottom of the screen that reads the aircraft's heading in degrees. The AI, which keeps the pilot straight and level during instrument flying, is so important that there are three of them: one in front of each pilot and a third, the older mechanical type, mounted low in the MD-11 at the center of the instrument panel, behind the throttles and thrust-reversers. It is designed to run off a reserve battery, which is constantly being recharged from the main power source. In light of the AI's later significance in the drama that resulted in the crash of Flight 111, an explanation as to the importance of this instrument—so important that three are provided—is in order.

When pilots are flying in conditions where they cannot see the ground, (for example at night, in cloud, in any bad weather conditions or all three), the AI gives reference to being level—or parallel to the ground. This becomes extremely important if pilots lose their automatic pilot—the system that automatically maintains the flight plan and coordinates—which is also directed by the AI through either a mechanical or computer-driven interface. Pilots are quite capable of flying without their auto pilot in darkness or bad weather conditions, but, without their AI or some other

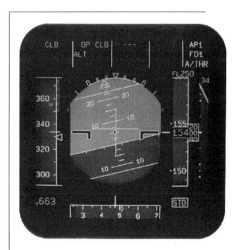

The Attitude Indicator (AI)—in this case a generic representation, part of the CRT display in front of the pilots. Speed display to the left, altimeter to the right and heading indicator on the bottom. This display indicates that the aircraft is in a slight climbing turn to the right at an altitude of 15,400 feet. The airplane is doing 335 knots and bearing 047 degrees magnetic.

reference to the Earth's surface, (such as a visual reference), they will invariably lose control of the aircraft. As we shall see, the outcome of the Swissair Flight 111 might have been entirely different had the pilots not lost their Primary Flight displays which include both the AI and the backup AI located behind the throttles low on the center console.

The other screens in front of Captain Zimmermann and First Officer Loëw displayed engine condition data such as temperature, engine rpms, exhaust gas temperatures, hydraulic pressures and fuel flow. Center of gravity was displayed, along with fuel management and fuel pump conditions. Communications equipment, navigational displays, and distance measurement were prominently displayed. Numerous enunciator lights, some of which doubled as push-type switches, were sprinkled across the panel. The computers on board Flight 111 were able to take most of the guesswork out of flying this airplane and were regarded as extra safety for both passengers and crew.

What the pilots could not possibly foresee was that massive and rapid electrical breakdown would occur less than an hour into their flight, stealing all of the safeguards technology had provided.

New York Center cleared Flight 111 from their control, handing it off to Boston Center. They exchanged pleasantries and guarded Boston's frequency (a pilot term, meaning to stay on the same frequency to listen) in case there was a need for their flight level or heading to be changed. Some time later there was a communication between Boston Center and Flight 111, ordering the pilots to change from the primary contacting frequency. There are several frequencies that Boston could have given Flight 111. The pilots rogered this instruction and complied, enjoyed a relatively quiet period with no further contact for about thirteen minutes. They didn't realize for some time that they were actually out of contact with Boston Center, whose controller could not reach them on the new frequency. It is not uncommon for a frequency to fail due to a faulty contact in the radio, and the pilots likely assumed that the new frequency was enjoying little or no radio traffic. It wasn't until they radioed Boston, some 13 minutes later, that they realized they were out of contact and switched back to the primary frequency and re-established contact. Though this was a curious event not long before Flight 111's trials began, there is no way of knowing if it was related to the horrendous problems that later arose. It's a fact of life in aviation that aircraft radios screw up from time to time, that's why most airplanes carry more than one. Still, as the transcript later shows, during the critical moments when the pilots were declaring an emergency, there is some question as to whether or not Moncton Center was getting the message.

The aircraft was by this time flying at its best cruise speed of .83 Mach which, at 33,000 ft, translates into a speed of about 1,060 kph, or 636 mph. (Because air density decreases with an increase in height, the speed of sound—on which Mach numbers are based—is greater at 33,000 feet than at sea level. Since air is thinner, the aircraft enjoys less drag as it pushes itself through the air; modern aircraft have equipment to compensate for this.) At its present speed, the MD-11 was theoretically covering ground at the rate of 17.6 km (10.6 mi) per minute. This speed does not take into account any influence on the aircraft from headwinds or tailwinds. Consequently, only fifty minutes into the flight the aircraft was crossing the southwestern portion of Nova Scotia on a track that would take it over the Atlantic Ocean and along the province's eastern coast.

One hour into its flight, at 9:58 P.M. local Nova Scotia time, Swissair Flight 111 made its first contact with Moncton Center in New Brunswick. The plane was now about two-thirds of the way across the Gulf of Maine and approximately 130 km (80 statute miles) southwest of Yarmouth Airport; the Boston Centre had handed control to the Moncton Center, and Zimmermann was apparently just checking in.

Everything seemed normal aboard the aircraft and the exchange was standard:

Flight 111: "Moncton Center: Swissair one-eleven heavy ("heavy" refers to the fact that the aircraft was a wide body jet) good evening, level three-three-zero." (31,000 feet)

Moncton controller: "Swissair one-eleven heavy, Moncton Center, good evening. Reports of occasional light turbulence at all levels."

The passengers aboard the aircraft were on New York time and so, probably, were their appetites. For them it was nearly nine o'clock in the Big Apple. The flight attendants were beginning their routine of pushing the meal carts along the narrow aisles and serving a late supper to the passengers, most of whom were now settling in for the long flight. Magazines and books were pulled from carry-on bags, a few laptop computers appeared and briefcases popped open. Postcards were filled out, letters were started, and entries were made in diaries.

Some of the passengers put on the sanitized headphones supplied by the airline and listened to the music or newscasts piped through to their respective armrests. Others experimented with a new state-of-the-art video entertainment system that had recently been installed by Interactive

Technologies Inc. in California. This touch-screen system supplied first and business class passengers with a personal video screen from which they could choose movies, video games, or music. And if the aircraft was outside areas where gambling was not permitted, passengers could use their credit cards to gamble on slot machines or play bingo. The master unit for this system was situated behind the rear flightdeck bulkhead and forward of the First Class passenger section. The new system was fed electrical power from one of the voltage busses below the floor of the cockpit in the electronic equipment bay. Those passengers using the entertainment system or enjoying the movies it provided were unaware that this piece of equipment would be the focus of an international investigation in the days and weeks to come. The investigation would drag on for over two years, targeting this non-essential entertainment system, and the wiring harness that fed it power, as the possible source of the fire that downed Flight 111, quite possibly costing its users—along with all other passangers and crew—their lives.

In the cockpit, the flight crew were enjoying their own meals while continuing to monitor the radio traffic between Moncton Centre and several other planes: a United Airlines flight, two British Airways Speedbird flights, and a Virgin Airlines Flight. During the exchanges, Captain Zimmermann noted an unusual odor in the cockpit—*smoke!* Zimmermann immediately appraised First Officer Loëw, who apparently was flying at the time, that he smelled smoke, and took control of the aircraft.

Smoke meant the real possibility of fire. And for a pilot, fire ranks right up there with engines quitting. In a closed environment, fire and its by-product, smoke, can be lethal. One can easily imagine what went through the minds of the flight crew when this first occurred. They had to consider immediately the consequences of an on-board fire, the real chance of a fuel explosion, and of the fire eating its way through the hull and being exposed to the hurricane-like slipstream outside—which would only increase its strength. Or the fire might find its way to a vital structural member, such as the main wing spar, where the blowtorch effect of wind could burn through the spar, causing the wing to fold like cardboard. Fire can burn through hydraulic lines, releasing fluids that add more fuel, helping to spread flames while at the same time taking away vital control functions or use of the landing gear. It can burn through wiring, robbing pilots of their instruments, igniting combustibles (such as carpets and the plastic liners around the inside of the hull) and creating toxic fumes. But probably the worst thing about an on-board fire is not knowing where it is.

Air-conditioning systems can pick up the smoky odour and spread it through the plane, and trying to locate the source is incredibly difficult. Unlike a landbound or seabound structure, the crew of an airliner can't just chop through walls in search of a fire's source; however, there are access hatches. Loëw hurriedly undid his seat belt and went to check the electronics bay under the floor just behind their seats to look for evidence of smoke or anything else that might be out of the ordinary. Located right below the floor of the flight deck in the MD-11, the equipment bay housed much of the sending units for data screens on the instrument panel, junction boxes, batteries, wire harnesses, and the oxygen bottles that fed the crew's oxygen masks. This area, sometimes called the "hell hole," was jammed in behind the nosewheel well and an after-bulkhead forward of the luggage compartment. Apparently finding nothing unusual, Loëw returned to his seat and informed Zimmermann that he could see nothing wrong in the electronics bay. Obviously concerned, Zimmermann called the senior flight attendant on the interphone and asked him to come to the flightdeck. The cabin crew was still in the process of serving supper. When the flight attendant arrived, he assured the Captain that he had not smelled smoke in the passenger compartment, but that he could smell it in the cockpit. A scan of the instruments available to Zimmermann and Loëw indicated no evidence of fire anywhere in the aircraft. In fact, when the Flight Data Recorder (FDR) was recovered after the crash, its data gave no indication of a fire anywhere on board the aircraft, even though there was evidence of extremely high temperatures in the cockpit, as well as testimony of witnesses to the crash—who described a bright light in the aircraft and along the wing, despite the fact that, by that time, all electrical power was down.

Probably relieved that the passenger compartment was normal, Zimmermann would still have been concerned with these phantom traces of smoke and the unmistakable odor of something burning. As a leaked tape of the conversation between the pilots later implies, the pilots first suspected the air conditioning system simply because air conditioners have long been a source of what at first appears to be smoke on the flight decks of airliners, when in reality it is only water vapor. In this case, it was an assumption that proved to distract the pilots, for critical minutes, from the real problem that was developing behind them, lurking in the baffling and plastic ceiling panels just behind the cockpit.

Once Captain Zimmermann could actually see the smoke he would know that he had a serious problem on his hands. His first concern was to find its source. Without knowing for sure what he was looking for, Zimmermann did what he and other pilots were trained to do: he reached for his procedures manual, a large, thick, looseleaf style binder with numerous sections and subsections, divided by tabs indicating the various sections relevant to trouble-shooting. One of these would undoubtedly detail the procedures to follow when there is evidence of smoke in the cockpit.

Zimmermann's second call to Moncton Centre, at 10:14 local time was vastly different from the one he made sixteen minutes earlier; he called in a Pan Pan Pan, and suggested he wanted to return to Boston.

Briefly, a Pan Pan Pan message by a pilot to any outside agency—whether it be to air traffic control or to all air traffic—is an indication that there is a problem on board the aircraft; however, it does not imply an emergency. Pilots know that minor problems on an airplane can escalate quickly to major ones, and they will usually alert air traffic control in the event that they are unable to do so if the problem escalates. For this reason, a Pan Pan Pan is not taken lightly. Ironically enough (especially in this case) it roughly equates to the old saying, "Where there's smoke there's fire." The difference between a Pan Pan Pan declaration and an emergency is that in an emergency the pilot can take whatever steps he thinks appropriate to get his aircraft safely on the ground without needing the consent of Air Traffic Control. Under the former, he is still under ATC's authority. Because the pilot had not declared an emergency, he was obliged to request permission to alter his flight pattern.

Moncton Centre was handling radio traffic from other aircraft when Zimmermann made his distress call. Terminal Control for Halifax International Airport (HIA), situated 35 km (22 mi) north of Halifax, is remotely directed from Moncton Center in New Brunswick, 170 km (106 mi) northwest of the airport, though the radar is located at HIA. However, Halifax maintains a Control Tower for traffic in its immediate area. The Moncton controller was just finishing an exchange with United Airlines Flight 920 and mentioned that "other airline is calling." The other aircraft was Swissair Flight 111; the busy Moncton controller had missed Swissair's identifier.

The only piece of hard evidence in the Swissair crash available within a matter of moments to any of the investigative bodies was the transcript of the conversation between Swissair and the Moncton controller, which was released to the media not long after the disaster. That transcript is reproduced below, along with explanations of aviation jargon, comments and analysis. All times are local.

Swissair 111 (10:14:18.0): "Swissair one-eleven heavy is declaring Pan Pan Pan. We have smoke in the cockpit. Request immediate return to a convenient place, I guess, Boston." By suggesting he return to Boston, Zimmermann is indicating that he wants to land the aircraft as quickly as possible.

Moncton controller (10:14:33.2): "Swissair one-eleven, roger...turn right proceed...you say to Boston you want to go."

Swissair 111 (10:14:33.2): "I guess Boston...we need first the weather so, we start a right turn here. Swissair one-one-one heavy."

Moncton controller (10:14:45.2): "Swissair one-eleven, roger, and a descent to flight level three-one-zero. Is that OK?"

Swissair 111 (10:14:50.3): "Three-one-zero." Here, Zimmermann's words obscured by the noise associated with donning oxygen masks. "Three-one-zero...one-one heavy."

The donning of oxygen masks when smoke is perceived or suspected is a precautionary procedure carried out on most airlines as a matter of course nowadays, regardless of how minor the problem might be. Swiftly-escalating problems might not allow the pilots to don masks in time, if the situation was to advance suddenly as the result of an explosion or fireball, for instance.

Moncton controller (10:15:03.1): "Swissair one-eleven, Center."

Swissair 111 (10:15:06.6): "Swissair one-eleven heavy, go ahead."

Moncton controller (10:15:08.6): "Would you prefer to go into Halifax?"

Swissair 111 (10:15:11.6): "Standby."

When Zimmermann declared Pan Pan Pan, Swissair 111 was in the vicinity of Yarmouth, Nova Scotia. It was 355 km from Boston airport but only 245 km from Halifax. Since Moncton Centre still had control over the aircraft's movements the reference to Halifax was more than a polite suggestion. Zimmermann's "standby" was probably to give him time to check his position and familiarize himself with his approach plates and database.

Swissair 111 (10:15:38.4): "Affirmative for Swissair one-eleven heavy. We prefer Halifax from our position."

It is important to understand the subtleties of protocol—based on mutual respect—that dictate the give-and-take between the pilot's right as captain of his aircraft and the controller's responsibilities over the airspace he controls. When Zimmermann made his Pan Pan Pan call, he was alerting the controller at Moncton, and anyone else guarding that frequency, that the situation aboard his aircraft was out of the ordinary, but he did not consider he had a full-scale emergency on his hands. The controller would then elevate Flight 111 status to keep a close eye on it and lend any requested assistance, while still maintaining control over its altitude and direction, particularly where it affected the flight levels and directions of other aircraft in Moncton's controlled airspace.

The controller at Moncton Center probably suggested landing in Halifax rather than Boston because it was closer, and he may have suspected that Zimmermann had no knowledge of the status of Halifax International as a viable alternative. There were, in fact, other alternatives as well: Yarmouth Airport, which Zimmermann had passed minutes earlier, and Greenwood Canadian Air Force Base, which was off his left wing about 120 km (70 mi) distant when he made his Pan Pan Pan call.

In any event, the flight crew had all of the necessary charts, called Jepperson plates, which are mandatory aboard a commercial aircraft. These provide hard-copy information in a flip-up ring binder about the sectors the aircraft might be required to fly. They are also available to the pilot in the aircraft database. Looking Halifax up in their IFR approach plates would have given the pilots information about the facilities available at Halifax, including landing and navigation aids, runway lengths, firefighting services, and the availability of medical aid. In this instance, Zimmermann asked one of the flight attendants to obtain the applicable sector plates from elsewhere in the aircraft because, under ordinary circumstances, the pilots would have had little need for them.

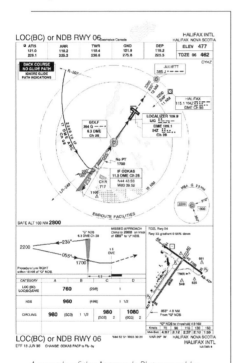

A sample of the Approach Plates used by pilots to familiarize themselves when landing at a controlled airport. In this case the plate is for Halifax International (CYHZ) in Nova Scotia. Runway layout is in the bottom right-hand corner.

Regardless, the controller in Moncton had solved a problem for Zimmermann and Loëw. By suggesting Halifax, the controller had given

Zimmermann a viable option which he was obliged to consider. Zimmermann, knowing that the controller would have a good working knowledge of the MD-11's emergency requirements and the ability of Halifax to handle them, confirmed his confidence in the controller's judgement by tacitly agreeing.

The transcript continues:

Moncton controller (10:15:43.8): "Swissair one-eleven, roger. Proceed direct to Halifax. Descend now to flight level two-niner-zero." (29,000 ft)

The air traffic controller had begun to set Flight 111 up for an approach into Halifax. Altitude, airspeed and the relationship between the two are critical to an approach to landing. The trick is to bleed off the airspeed and the tendency for an aircraft to increase its speed during descent, so that the aircraft arrives at the threshold of the runway at the right height and airspeed for landing.

Swissair 111 (10:15:48.7): "Level two-niner-zero to Halifax, Swissair one-eleven heavy."

The pilot or co-pilot will always read back to the controller any instruction received so the controller knows that the pilot has heard the message and understands it. This holds true with any aircraft—private, commercial, or military—in controlled airspace.

BAW Speedbird 214 (10:15:58.3): "Swissair one-eleven heavy, from Speedbird two-one-four, I can give you the Halifax weather if you like."

Though pilots don't usually chatter on frequencies assigned to them by the sector controller, they will do so in a situation where pilots think they might be able to assist other pilots during a crisis. The controller might reign them in after a point or get them to change to another frequency.

BAW Speedbird knew that to get the weather for Halifax, Zimmermann would have to change frequencies to 126.7 Mhz, Halifax Flight Service Station (called Halifax Radio) or listen to the Automated Tower Information Service (ATIS) on 121.0 for an abbreviated weather announcement, both of which would take time and attention from the situation at hand. In a crisis situation, speed in acquiring information is important. Speedbird is guessing that the pilots already have their hands full and hopes to simplify things for them.

Swissair 111 (10:16:04.1): "Swissair one-eleven heavy, we have the oxygen mask on. Go ahead with the weather.

Zimmermann is likely indicating that he thinks the situation is serious enough to warrant the use of the oxygen masks and also that communications from that point on might prove more difficult or garbled.

BAW Speedbird 214 (10:16:10.4): "OK, it's the three hundred Zulu weather was one-zero-zero at niner knots, one-five miles, scattered at one-two-zero, broken at two-five-zero, plus seventeen, plus twelve, two-niner-eight-zero, over."

The "Zulu weather" means the Universal Corrected Time (UCT) weather, i.e., the time in Greenwich, England, through which the Prime Meridian passes. For years it was called Zulu time and was changed to UCT several years ago to satisfy political wrangling. Many pilots still refer to it as Zulu time. Had the local time been "standard time" there would have been a four-hour difference from Greenwich Time, but because "daylight saving time" was in effect there was only a three-hour lag behind Greenwich Time. At Halifax the winds were at 100 degrees magnetic at 9 knots (17.5 kph or 10.5 mph), visibility was 25 km(15 mi). There were scattered clouds at 25,000 ft, 17,000 ft, 12,000 ft The barometric pressure was at 29.80 inches of mercury. In aviation lingo, the last two zeros are always dropped from the weather reports involving altitude and flight levels. For example, Flight Level 290 means the level at an altitude of 29,000 ft.

As we will learn later, one of the most distressing facts of this terrible drama was that the weather over Halifax was considerably better than over St. Margarets Bay. Had different decisions been made, the good weather at Halifax alone could have saved the day.

Swissair 111 (10:16:29.8): "Roger, Swissair one-eleven heavy. We copy the altimeter is two-niner-eight-zero."

Moncton controller (10:16:38.6): "Swissair one-eleven, you're cleared to 10,000 ft and the Hal-...altimeter is two-nine-eight-zero."

Controllers are always updating the barometric pressure so that the pilots can reset their altimeters.

Swissair 111 (10:16:41.7): "Two-niner-eight zero, 10,000 ft, Swissair one-eleven heavy."

Moncton controller (10:16:52.5): "And Swissair one-eleven, can you tell me what your fuel on board is and the number of passengers?"

This information would have been flashed to Halifax to the firefighting services and for ambulance evacuation purposes, should they be needed.

Swissair 111 (10:16:58.3): "Roger, standby for this."

Zimmermann needed some time to update the data because the fuel state was constantly changing. As it turned out, the discussion concerning fuel, when it did take place, resulted in the most critical decision that Zimmermann would ever make.

BAW Speedbird 1506 (10:17:15.5): "Speedbird one-five-zero six is at Tusky listening out."

Moncton controller (10:17:19.3): "Speedbird one-five-zero-six, roger."

BAW Speedbird might have been giving the Moncton controller a subtle reminder that this scenario was unfolding on a frequency used to direct traffic through Moncton Center's sector. This seems to be borne out by the Moncton controller's next transmission.

Moncton controller (10:18:19.3): "Swissair one-eleven, you can contact Moncton Center now one-one-niner-point-two."

The Moncton controller has handed off Flight 111 to Terminal Control, situated elsewhere in the room, so that he could continue working other aircraft overflying their sector such as the British AirWays Speedbird and Virgin Airlines.

Moncton Center is located just outside Moncton, New Brunswick,and assumes routing responsibility for all air traffic above 12,500 feet, both within and travelling through its sector. All major airport traffic in its area is controlled from Moncton to within a prescribed distance to that airport.

On the other hand, Halifax International Airport has its own tower personnel who control traffic only within a seven mile radius of the tower and up to an altitude of 3,500 feet. Though the rotating radar antennae which paints the aircraft target is located near Halifax, its signal is piped through to Moncton via cable where it is monitored by two different controllers—first the Sector Controller, who handles traffic passing through the sector, and then the Terminal Control Controller, who assumes responsibility for directing aircraft 35 miles from the airport if those planes are going to land at Halifax. This controller directs the aircraft until it reaches the seven-mile radius Control Zone at Halifax where it is once more handed off to the Halifax Tower controller for the actual landing.

Swissair 111 (10:18:24.4): "One-one-niner-point-two for the Swissair one-one-one heavy."

Moncton controller (10:18:31.0): "Roger."

The Halifax Terminal controller in Moncton, presumably advised of the situation aboard Flight 111 and the Pan Pan Pan, assumes control of directing the MD-11 into Halifax airport.

Swissair 111 (10:18:34.3): "Moncton Center, good evening. Swissair one-eleven heavy, flight level two-five-four descending flight level two-five-zero on course Halifax. We are flying at the time on track zero-five-zero." (Heading of 50 degrees magnetic.)

Halifax controller (10:18:46.8): "Swissair one-eleven, good evening. Descend to 3,000 the altimeter is two-nine-seven-nine."

The altimeter is constantly updated as the pressure at Halifax changes.

Swissair 111 (10:18:51.8): "We would prefer at the time around 8,000 ft, two-nine-eight-zero, until the cabin is ready for the landing."

Halifax controller (10:19:00:9): "Swissair one-eleven, you can descend to three, level off at an intermediate altitude if you wish. Just advise."

Swissair 111 (10:19:07.2): "Roger. At the time we descend to 8,000 ft We are anytime clear to 3,000. I keep you advised."

Halifax controller (10:19:14.5): "OK, can I vector you to set up for runway zero-six at Halifax?"

Swissair 111 (10:19:19.4): "Say again latest wind, please."

Halifax controller (10:19:22.1): "OK, active runway Halifax zero-six. Should I start you on a vector for six?"

As indicated by BAW Speedbird earlier, the winds were at 100 degrees magnetic so the obvious choice is Runway 06 at Halifax, giving the aircraft landing there a 40 degree quartering crosswind from the right. Crosswinds are not usually as significant for large and heavy aircraft unless the winds are strong. A wind coming from one side of the aircraft tends to increase the lift of the wing on that side, while the wing on the other side is robbed of that lift by the blanketing effect of the aircraft's fuselage. The pilot corrects for this by holding down the wing receiving direct wind and crabbing into the wind (flying slightly sideways while still moving in the intended direction) to avoid the low wing from hitting the ground. Runway numbers indicate their magnetic heading; i.e., runway 06 means 060 degrees magnetic.

Swissair 111 (10:19:26.3): "Yes, vector for six will be fine. Swissair one-eleven heavy."

Halifax controller (10:19:31.0): "Swissair one-eleven, roger. Turn left heading of zero-three-zero."

Swissair 111 (10:19:35.1): "Left heading zero-three-zero for the Swissair one-eleven."

Halifax controller (10:19:39.5): "OK, it's a back course approach for runway zero-six. The localizer frequency one-zero-niner-decimal-niner. You've got 30 mi to fly to the threshold." (End of the runway, sometimes called the button.)

Swissair 111 (10:19:53.3): "We need more than 30 miles. Please, say me again the frequency of the back beam."

Zimmermann obviously figured that he needed more than thirty miles to lose altitude and speed and possibly to bleed off some of his fuel.

Halifax controller (10:19:59.5): "Swissair one-eleven, roger. You can turn left heading three-six-zero to lose some altitude, the frequency is one-zero-niner-decimal-niner for the localizer. It's a back course approach."

Swissair 111 (10:20:09.5): "One-zero-niner-point-niner, roger. And we are turning left to heading north. Swissair one-eleven heavy."

Dinner is still being served in the cabin, and Zimmermann instructs the flight attendant to announce to the passengers that the

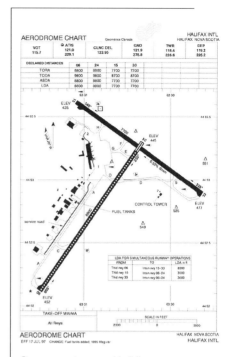

Runways, taxiways and buildings at Halifax International Airport.

plane is going to land in Halifax in twenty to twenty-five minutes. Meanwhile, the captain has begun an emergency checklist trying to find the source of the smoke. In cases where electrical fire is suspected, any power busses not required are shut down, and the first step is to disconnect power to the cabin, leaving just emergency lighting in the back of the plane. Flight attendants are advised that power will be shut off and are told to use flashlights to collect meal trays. Flight attendants report to Captain Zimmermann that the passengers are relatively calm. Passengers are also instructed to don their personal flotation devices—a standard procedure—but nevertheless a potentially disturbing one.

Halifax controller (10:21:23.1): "Swissair one-eleven, when you have time could I have the number of souls on board and your fuel on board please for emergency services."

Swissair 111 (10:21:30.1): "Roger. At the time fuel on board is two-three-zero tons. We must dump some fuel. May we do that in this area during descent?"

Although it must have occurred to Zimmermann that he would have to dump some fuel before attempting to land at Halifax, he had probably been pre-occupied with other problems, since he never did respond to the Moncton controller's question five minutes earlier, "Can you tell me what your fuel on board is...." Although the fuel no doubt was a concern, he needed time to set up his approach and, since he was still in a Pan Pan Pan situation, he would need permission to dump wherever he was.

Two three zero tons represents the current gross weight of the aircraft, not the amount of fuel on board. In the wake of the crash, there is ongoing debate as to whether the MD-11 could have landed safely at Halifax International at its current weight. Swissair, which later simulated the flight and conditions, contends the plane could not have landed safely. Pilots familiar with the MD-11 and manufacturer's gross landing weight argue a safe landing was quite feasible.

Halifax controller (10:21:40.9): "OK, I am going to take you...Are you able to take a turn back to the south or do you want to stay closer to the airport?"

Swissair 111 (10:21:47.0): "Standby short, standby short."

Zimmermann probably wanted time to consider whether the situation was now serious enough to dump fuel over the Halifax Peninsula, or whether he had time to turn south to dump over water.

Swissair 111 (10:21:59.1): "OK, we are able for a left or right turn towards the south to dump."

Halifax controller (10:22:04.2): "Swissair one-eleven, roger, turn to the left, heading of two-zero-zero degrees and advise time when you are ready to dump. It will be about 10 miles. before you are off the coast. You are still within about 25 miles of the airport."

The controller appears to be giving a subtle reminder to Zimmermann that though he's now only 25 miles from the threshold of runway 06, by turning south he will increase his distance from HIA by another ten miles. This was a critical moment in the flight: Zimmermann elected to turn the aircraft away from Halifax International Airport.

Swissair 111 (10:22:20.3): "Roger, we are turning left and in that case we're descending at the time only to 10,000 ft to dump the fuel."

Halifax controller (10:22:29.6): "OK, maintain one-zero-thousand. I'll advise you when you are over the water and it will be very shortly."

Swissair 111 (10:22:34.4): "Roger."

Swissair 111 (10:22:36.2): (First Officer Loëw, depressing the wrong transmit button, asks Zimmermann,) *"Du bisch in der* emergency checklist *für* air conditioning smoke?" (Are you in the emergency checklist for air conditioning smoke?)

Loëw, his eyes probably locked on his instruments, is no doubt wondering what part of the procedures manual Zimmermann is consulting. Since air conditioning—a culprit in many such cases of smoke—was their first suspicion, Loëw is asking the captain if this is still his opinion.

Halifax controller (10:22:42.9): "Swissair one-eleven, say again please."

Swissair 111 (10:22:45.3): "Ah, sorry, it was not for you. Swissair one-eleven was asking internally. It was my fault, sorry about."

This last exchange might be a telling incident. Radio transmissions in most aircraft are controlled by a button on the control column, normally accessible to the pilot's thumb. Depressing this push-to-talk (PTT) switch allows the pilot to transmit, and the radio will not receive until the button is released. Even if there is no verbal transmission, the carrier wave being transmitted will prevent other aircraft radios in the vicinity from transmitting on the same frequency. It is a source of embarrassment to most pilots to have depressed the PTT while making comments not meant to go out over the radio. This error happens to pilots in a variety of circumstances; for example, when a pilot is stressed or distracted during a crisis, or when he is bombarded with excessive information. A change to routine, such as wearing oxygen masks, could be a sufficient distraction.

The Emergency Oxygen System in use on Flight 111 automatically changed the intercom system between the two pilots to a live system, without them having to push a button, thus allowing the men to converse freely (or as freely as you can with a mask over your face). By depressing the Microphone Activation Switch on their control yokes, they could then transmit over the VHF radios. For some unknown reason, Zimmermann transmitted his words to both Loëw and Moncton Center.

Halifax controller (10:22:50.8): "OK."

Halifax controller (:23:33.1): "Swissair one-eleven continue left heading one-eight-zero. You'll be off the coast in about 15 miles."

Swissair 111 (10:23:39.2): "Roger, heading left one-eight-zero. Swissair one-eleven and maintaining at 10,000 ft."

Halifax controller (10:23:46.3): "Roger."

Halifax controller (10:23:55.7): "You will be staying within about 35, 40 miles of the airport if you have to get to the airport in a hurry."

Swissair 111 (10:24.03.9): "OK, that's fine for us. Please tell me when we can start to dump the fuel."

Halifax controller (10:24:08.8): "OK."

Swissair 111 (10:24:28.1): (Background phone) "Swissair one-eleven. At the time we must fly manually. Are we cleared to fly between ten thou...11,000 and 9,000 ft.?" (Sound of auto pilot disconnect warbler.) This is the first indication of a malfunction in the computer which runs the auto pilot. The AI must still be functioning since Zimmermann still knows his attitude.

Halifax controller (10:24:28.1): "Swissair one-eleven, you can block between 5,000 and 12,000 if you wish."

Three seconds later both pilots of Swissair declare an emergency.

Swissair 111 (10:24:45.1): "Swissair one-eleven heavy is declaring emergency. (10:24:46.4 second voice overlap) Roger, we are between 12,000 and 5,000 ft. We are declaring emergency now at time, zero-one-two." Having declared an emergency—from now on—the sky is Zimmermann's domain. He is no longer required to ask Moncton Air Control for permission to take any action he considers prudent to safely land his aircraft. He alone must make the decisions—decisions which will affect every person on board the aircraft, as well as thousands of others, who continue to live with the aftermath of this overwhelming tragedy.

Halifax controller (10:24:56.0): "Roger."

Swissair 111 (10:24:56.5): "Eleven heavy, we starting dump now, we have to land immediate."

Halifax controller (10:25:00.7): "Swissair one-eleven, just a couple of miles, I'll be right with you."

Either the Halifax controller is saying it is only a couple of miles to the airport and that he will stay in constant communication, or, judging from this response, he had not actually heard Zimmermann declare an emergency. He might have been talking on another frequency (the controllers at Moncton need only press a button to go to another frequency).

Swissair 111 (10:25:04.1): "Roger." (Sound, probably auto pilot disconnect warbler.)

Then, possibly because the pilots realized that Halifax Control didn't receive their message, both pilots scramble for the radio to declare an emergency, saying again they have to land immediately. Their data recorder picks up problems with flight control computer and other systems.

Swissair 111 continues (10:25:05.4): "And we are declaring emergency now, Swissair one-eleven."

Halifax controller (10:25:08.6): "Copy that."

Halifax controller (10:25:19.2): "Swissair one-eleven, you are cleared to commence your fuel dump on that track and advise me when the dump is complete."

For some reason the Halifax controller continues to be preoccupied with the fuel dump despite the fact that Zimmermann has now told him twice that he is declaring an emergency and the transmission has been acknowledged. The fuel dump is no longer the controller's responsibility and, if anything, must be a distraction from the real emergency facing the pilots. Zimmermann could have been dumping fuel all the way into Halifax if he needed to.

Cockpit Voice Recorder (CVR) Item (10:25:41:00): Loëw reports to Zimmermann that he has lost all his main instruments. Data and voice recorders quit working.

Halifax controller (10:25:43.0): "Swissair one-eleven, check you're cleared to start the fuel dump."

Swissair 111 (10:25:49.3): Unintelligible response. There is no further communication with Air Traffic Control.

Despite Air Traffic Control's repeated attempts to contact Flight 111, silence prevailed. The cockpit crew likely could not respond.

Although the aircraft's Mode C transponder codes, which give the aircraft's location, identifier, and attitude, had disappeared from Moncton Control's screen, the primary radar revealed that the target was still there. The radar site at Halifax was painting an image that was still tracking southward over St. Margarets Bay, parallel to the eastern coast of the Aspotogan Peninsula.

Radio communications with Flight 111 ended abruptly when the aircraft was 2 km (1.6 mi) east of Birchy Head on the Aspotogan Peninsula. The controllers at Moncton Center watched, perplexed, as the aircraft continued to the south, swinging in close to the Halifax peninsula, travelling parallel to and in close to the shore at Indian Harbour on the northeast side of the bay before turning once more out over the Atlantic Ocean. Obviously the pilots still had manual control of the aircraft. Why, then, had they not turned toward the airport and the emergency crews they knew would be waiting?

The FDR recording found after the crash confirmed what the cockpit transcripts suggested—that there were problems with the flight control computer and other crucial systems. What the recordings couldn't record was the drama unfolding in the cockpit as the two pilots tried to deal with a massive, fuel heavy aircraft, flying at 610 kph with no instrumentation—no way of knowing where they were, their angle of flight through the air, or how long they had left before smoke or fire overcame them.

At Indian Harbour, Shirley and Harry Publicover had just arrived home. Standing next to their car, Harry remembers seeing the jet travelling over their house at an estimated altitude of 100 ft. (This is likely an error because Halifax was still painting the MD-11 on its primary radar, and it couldn't see below 610 ft.) Strangely, Publicover recalls that the aircraft was not showing any lights outside; however, he insists, "...inside she was lit up like a hotel. You could almost see the passengers." He remarked to his wife, "My God, that shouldn't be like that." It is difficult to imagine how the aircraft could be lit up inside since there was apparently no power to provide the voltage necessary to run the cabin lights. There is no evidence that fire had broken out in the cabin. My only explanation is that there was an electrical glitch, caused by the havoc taking place in the miles of electric wiring throughout the plane, that either triggered the cabin lights, or caused the phenomenon described by Publicover. Residents of St. Margarets Bay are used to seeing many of the one thousand aircraft that pass overhead day and night, either travelling on the overseas-international route, making approaches into Halifax International Airport or into Canadian Forces Base, Shearwater on the other side of the Halifax peninsula and across the harbour from the port city. The difference on this occasion was the altitude of the aircraft. It was low enough to impress Publicover, low enough that the engines' roar was almost deafening, and low enough to smell the fuel being dumped overboard. Publicover may not have known that the passengers and crew of Flight 111 had less than four minutes left to live, but he would not have been surprised; the crash of a large, fully-loaded aircraft into the sea is a recipe for disaster.

Off Middle Point, just south of Indian Harbour, Flight 111 began a long sweeping turn to the right, taking it on a course out past East Ironbound Island and between East Ironbound and Pearl (Green) Islands. There it continued on a westerly heading for about thirty seconds before swinging back to the northwest, then to the north, where it passed to the east of Big and Little Tancook Islands. Now the aircraft continued northeasterly and then easterly, crossing the tip of the Aspotogan Peninsula over Blandford and eventually the Bayswater area. Gradually, Flight 111 was completing a large oval pattern that was about 13 km (8 mi) across. Past Bayswater, it swung more sharply to the southeast, continuing on that course for several kilometres.

It has been mentioned that there was a cloud cover over St. Margarets Bay at about 2,000 feet, but that Publicover actually saw the aircraft through a break in the clouds. We know from Zimmermann's own words that the pilots were flying the plane manually, perhaps hoping to make a crash landing into the ocean. But even to crash land they needed to find a point of reference; a beacon by which they could judge if they were flying level and horizontal. There were several such beacons precisely in their convoluted path: the lighthouses scattered around the Bay.

Then, about 11 km (7 mi) southwest of Peggys Cove, everything went wrong. Possibly the crew lost manual control of the aircraft; possibly, in a mad chase for a light, they lost sight of their only hope in the cloud cover; or, possibly they could no longer see.

For whatever reason, at about 800 ft above the Atlantic, the jetliner abruptly rolled over on its back then dove inverted

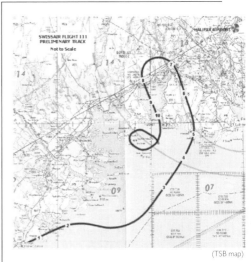

(TSB map)

The Flight Track of Swissair 111 as generated by the Transportation Safety Board of Canada. Note number ten is the last communication point with FL-111.

and nearly vertically into the sea. The nose of the aircraft slammed into a shoal about 15 m (40 ft) below the surface, while the rear of the aircraft was blasted into hundreds of thousands of tiny pieces. The sound of the blast ricocheted around the rocky coast and off the cloud layers above. Then silence washed like the waves of the Atlantic over the shattered remains of Swissair Flight 111.

David Hirtle, an electrician, and his wife Hazel live in the picturesque village of Blandford, a community of only a few hundred on the southwestern tip of the Aspotogan Peninsula. Like many other Nova Scotia fishing communities, Blandford boasts a Government Wharf with a complement of colourful fishing boats, a fish plant, several picture-postcard churches, and friendly people. The latter would become evident when the little community would be jolted out of obscurity into headlines and onto television screens around the world.

On September 2, at about 10:30 P.M. local time, David and Hazel were watching television in the front room. It had been an eventful day—they had dropped their son off at Halifax International Airport for a flight to Toronto and had just returned home. Hazel heard a sound similar to what she later described as "tires crunching on the gravel driveway" on the south side of their house. It was "a [very loud] crackling type of noise."

Curious, she mentioned it to her husband then went to the back door to see if anyone had driven into the driveway. There was nothing to see. David followed her into the kitchen because he too could hear what sounded like an "airplane descending to land." He walked out to the patio and looked up. At first he could see nothing because the sky was cloudy, but almost directly overhead he could hear the increasingly loud roar of an airplane.

Suddenly, out of the low cloud layer the belly of the aircraft came into view; it was reportedly bathed in a yellow glow. Though David could not see the jets of the aircraft, he could hear them whining. He watched the aircraft for about seven seconds as it crossed overhead and swiftly disappeared into another cloud layer to the east of him. He watched and listened for several more seconds before going back inside.

"That airplane is going down," he remarked to Hazel. He no sooner uttered the words when they both heard a loud thud.

A few hundred feet to the southeast of the Hirtle residence, Brenda Murphy was also watching television when she heard an airplane approaching. The noise it made was so loud it shook her mobile home. Brenda immediately went to look out a window and spotted an airplane, at an altitude which she estimated at 800 ft, heading in the direction of Peggys Cove. Her first thought was, My God, this plane is in trouble. She later told reporters, "There was a glow from the left wing back and flames in front of the left wing. The whole plane was not on fire. I had a very clear view." She guessed that about a minute passed before she heard what sounded like two eighteen-wheelers travelling at high speed, crashing head-on.

A little further to the east, in the village of Bayswater, Glenda Reid and her mother both heard a low-flying aircraft. Glenda said it sounded like it was flying over the house and a lot lower than usual. Her mother heard sounds "like car doors slamming" as the jet flew over their house. Also in Bayswater, Alberta Martin reported that she heard a low-flying aircraft and then a thunderous explosion. Doris Murphy heard the aircraft when it passed south of Northwest Cove, and thought it sounded as though it were having engine trouble. In Glen Margaret, on the east side of St. Margarets Bay, Rita Westhaver thought she heard a loud clap of thunder, but thought nothing more of it until her son, a paramedic, received a call at their home asking him to report to work. He told her there was a general call out for paramedics because an airliner had crashed somewhere off Peggys Cove.

While people in coastal Nova Scotia villages glimpsed the MD-11 approaching its tragic end, the Moncton and Halifax controllers tried repeatedly but unsuccessfully to raise Flight 111. There was nothing yet to indicate that the aircraft had crashed, because the Halifax-based radar painted its target for several more minutes. However, there was enough concern to call the Rescue Coordination Center (RCC) at the Canadian naval base at Stadacona in Halifax. Moncton Center advised RCC that although Flight 111 was still on their radar, it was in difficulty and they had lost radio contact with the aircraft.

Flight 111 was lost from radar contact somewhere between five and six minutes after the last transmission. Seconds later, at 10:31:30 a seismic station maintained by Dalhousie University in Halifax registered an event measuring one on the Richter scale. Though unaware of this fact at the time, the Moncton controller made another call to the RCC to advise that they had lost radar contact with Flight 111 at an altitude of 800 ft., and they suspected the aircraft might have gone into the water somewhere off the Aspotogan Peninsula, about 40 nautical miles southeast of Halifax International Airport. It had been in the air fifteen minutes, after first declaring a Pan Pan Pan travelling at an approximate speed of 600 kph and was hardly any closer to the Halifax tarmac and safety.

The lighthouse on East Ironbound Island, 3 km due south of the tip of the Aspotogan Peninsula, has a commanding view of the ocean and the approaches to St. Margarets Bay, and guards the entrance to Mahone Bay. Trish and Phil Hughes, the only year-round inhabitants on the barely mile-long island, had already turned in for the evening. Trish was awakened by the sound of a low-flying jet passing so close overhead that their house rattled from the engines. Fumes from Flight 111's fuel dumping permeated her bedroom. Not long after, the couple heard a very short, sharp explosion.

Trish hurriedly pulled on a pair of jogging pants and ran to the lighthouse, perched on the island's highest point, 35 m above the sea. She looked just north of eastward toward the winking beacon of Peggys Light across the lonely, empty expanse of water. Although she didn't really expect to see anything—when she heard the explosion she knew there wouldn't be any survivors—she could never have imagined what was about to happen. In just a few hours, these waters would become one of the busiest and most congested areas on the eastern seaboard of Nova Scotia, when searchers would come out in great numbers, full of hope, to rescue. Nor could she have anticipated the awful flotsam that would fetch up on their tiny island several hours later.

CHAPTER TWO

The Search for Survivors

Night: The Search Begins

Following Swissair Flight 111's emergency call, the firefighters of Halifax International Airport's emergency co-ordination center were in place within five minutes of receiving the call from Moncton Centre to activate. The airport maintains an emergency response service twenty-four hours a day, seven days a week and have responded to many such calls. They waited anxiously for the arrival of Swissair Flight 111, but they would wait in vain.

The Rescue Coordination Center (RCC) in Halifax received its first call from Moncton Center after it lost Flight 111 off its primary radar in Halifax at 10:31 P.M. They were advised that an aircraft was probably down in the ocean off St. Margarets Bay. For more than forty years, RCC Halifax has been handling distress calls from fishing boats, yachts and other pleasure boats, container ships, small vessels such as offshore trawlers and draggers, and, from time to time, a light aircraft that has ditched in the North Atlantic. To deal with an average of 2,200 incidents a year, RCC is operated by a rotating staff of military personnel from all areas of the armed forces. (Staffing depends on the circumstances, but usually a visitor would find five to six people in the Center on a "normal" day.)

Fortunately, only a small percentage of the calls to RCC escalate into large-scale emergencies. But when they do, RCC has a myriad of resources and assets that can be brought into play. These include well-trained military (air, sea, land) and paramilitary Search and Rescue (SAR) personnel such as the Coast Guard, Department of Fisheries and Oceans vessels crew, the RCMP, local police and fire departments and civilian SAR agencies such as the ground SAR and the Canadian Coast Guard Auxiliary (CCGA), made up of volunteers from the fishing and pleasure boat communities). There are additional ships, aircraft, transport vehicles, and other equipment available to RCC, as required. Perhaps because Nova Scotia has had more than its share of disasters, and because Halifax is a navel base and military base, these resources are abundant.

Maj. Michel Brisebois, the Officer-in-Charge (OIC) at RCC Halifax, had been home from work only fifteen minutes when, at 11:10 P.M., he received a call from RCC asking him to return. All hell had broken loose in the operations center.

A first-time visitor to the RCC operations center is usually underwhelmed. The op-center is nothing more than a plain square room, with three desks and consoles facing a large map of the RCC's vast area of responsibility, which stretches well north to include the eastern half of Quebec, then further east to Iceland down the middle of the Atlantic Ocean and back to the American-Canadian border. Little cutouts like fridge magnets line the left side of the map and are affixed to various positions on the chart, indicating the number and types of available assets and their current location and activity. An "asset" is RCC jargon for naval and Coast Guard vessels, small boats, airplanes and helicopters, troops and civilian SAR personnel, for example. On the wall opposite the map is a large wall chart with currently-available assets, their location or possible maintenance situation. Aircraft are always in one maintenance mode or other while aero-mechanical engineers look into snags (small problems such as intermittent radios, intercom problems, minor hydraulic leaks) or perform regular 25-, 50-, or 100-hour (flying time) inspections.

The consoles contain bookshelves, a computer, and a clutch of telephones with speed dials. There are other desks or higher tables with shelves holding sea charts in varying scales of resolution, each coded to a particular sector of coastline or land area in the Halifax sector.

When Major Brisebois arrived back at the operations center, the phones were ringing off the hook and had been for over a half-hour. The flood of incoming calls from around the world, mostly the press seeking information, was preventing RCC from using the their phones to mount a search-and-rescue operation for Swissair. Brisebois was shocked at how fast the media had been alerted to the crash off Peggys Cove. To make matters worse, there were initially only three people on duty.

Within an hour Maj. Brisebois had twelve personnel working to get the situation under control. A Search Master—an experienced person in search and rescue—was assigned to each key area of the crisis and charged with the responsibility of controlling only that situation, thereby narrowing their focus and allowing greater attention to detail. Though RCC still had several dedicated land-line links such as the one connecting them to Coast Guard Radio Halifax, their first priority was to tackle the problem of the jammed phone lines. Sixteen personnel, drawn from the Canadian Navy and RCC public affairs sections, were given the task of moving media traffic from vital RCC communications lines to an alternate communications centre, localizing the flow to a single point of contact and information. This was called the Information Command Structure and was comprised of key people from Swissair, the RCMP, Emergency Measures Organization (EMO), and the Canadian Coast Guard. Since each organization had its own emergency unit, they were easily linked together by telephone hook-ups and data links.

Meanwhile, the primary RCC team was doing what it was created to do: coordinate the search and rescue for Flight 111, named Operation Persistence, the morning after the crash. First, though, they had to locate the point of impact. They began with the Last Known Position (LKP) of the aircraft supplied by Moncton Center. Moncton had lost Flight 111 at an altitude of 800 ft. off the primary radar in Halifax. Given the direction of the flight reports via 911 calls, and direct calls to RCC from residents on the tip of the Aspotogan Peninsula, they plotted an area on their charts of 10 square nautical miles surrounding the LKP, which was at 44:23 N latitude and 63:56 W longitude, 7 nautical miles dead south of Peggys Light.

Although RCC maintains tight control of any event, their personnel do not talk directly to the assets involved in a search. This is done through intermediary agencies and an on-scene-commander. In this case, the OSC seconded for the task was Capt. Rick Town from HMCS *Preserver*, a navy supply ship based in Halifax, and the agencies were the Canadian Coast Guard and Federal Fisheries vessels, the RCMP, the Canadian Air Force, and the Canadian Navy. These four agencies would each contact their own assets, as well as assets assigned to them by RCC. For example, the RCMP would not only deal with their own personnel but would take responsibility for directing Nova Scotia's Emergency Measures Organization, which in turn would direct the Ground Search Units, and the medical assets (including air medevac units, ambulances and paramedics), and would organize whatever hospital arrangements they anticipated would be required. Within two hours, thousands of people were involved in the search for and the preparation to receive survivors.

By the time RCC had con-tacted Coast Guard Radio Hali-fax to advise them that there were strong suspicions that a commercial airline had crashed off the mouth of St. Margarets Bay, Coast Guard vessels *Earl Gray* and *Mary Hitchens* were al-ready steaming to the presumed site of the impact. A few min-utes before RCC's call, Coast Guard Radio Halifax had re-ceived a radio transmission from Granville Cleveland, a Blandford

(DND photo)

The Canadian Navy's supply ship HMCS Preserver served as a floating morgue and a debris collection point during the initial days after the crash of Swissair Flight 111.

fisherman who reported that an aircraft had just flown very low over his residence and that it was "desperate loud." Then, he said, he heard the en-gines whine to a higher pitch and heard a loud crash. This had galvanized the Coast Guard into action. After contacting the Coast Guard, RCC made a blanket call for assistance at 10:49 p.m, requesting vessels in the area to proceed to the estimated crash site to aid in the recovery of survivors.

Immediately after Rescue Coordination Centre had transmitted the coordinates of Flight 111's last known position, they received a radio transmission from Neil Hughes, the skipper of the fishing vessel *Jennifer and Jean* informing them that he was outbound for the area. Shortly after, the cruise ship *Nantucket Clipper* called in to advise that they too were proceeding to the area to offer assistance. The Canadian Navy was in-volved in an exercise thirty nautical miles southeast of that position and responded to the call, as did Canadian Fisheries and Coast Guard vessels. The Halifax Class frigate *Ville de Quebec* and HMCS *Preserver*, with Cap. Rick Town on board, were steaming to the area, joining the Coast Guard cutter *Sambro*, which was close to the scene early on.

The Canadian Coast Guard Auxiliary—a volunteer organization com-prised mostly of fishing boats from local fishing communities—was alerted by RCC, who requested six boats for the search. However, many other local fisherman and owners of pleasure boats, hearing of the disaster on their home-based marine band radios, took it upon themselves to put to sea and help. Dozens sailed out of the fishing ports, coves, and harbours scattered along the South Shore of Nova Scotia, from Sambro to Chester, heading for the mouth of St. Margarets Bay.

Sea King helicopters from nearby Shearwater Naval Airbase, C-130 Hercules aircraft, and Labrador helicopters from CFB Greenwood were immediately dispatched to the scene. The hospitals in Halifax and Dartmouth were put on alert and, initially, fourteen ambulances were posted along the south shore of St. Margarets Bay, and the total soon rose to forty. Paramedics from as far away as Digby, Nova Scotia, were dispatched to the site by the RCMP.

Although local television broadcasts were indicating that the Swissair aircraft might have ditched in relatively calm seas off the mouth of St. Margarets Bay, the weather in the area on that night was not good. Hurricane Danielle had passed through not long before, leaving heavy seas with up to 1.5-m (5-ft.) waves and winds gusting up to 25 knots. Driving ran and fog patches reduced visibility to 10 m (30 ft.) in any direction. Despite the marginal weather, military helicopters, such as the Sea Kings and Labradors, along with a couple of C-130 Hercules out of Greenwood, were soon over the presumed crash site. They were dropping flares and lighting the surface of the water with powerful searchlights. Flares drifted down from the sky, rocking under their little parachutes, casting flickering orange-tinged shadows on the water below.

It was hazardous out on the water that night. There was real danger of some of the smaller vessels swamping in the heavy chop, or being run down or hit by another boat in poor visibility. Fortunately, the fishermen were experienced sailors, well acquainted with the hazards of the unpredictable and unforgiving North Atlantic. It was probably helpful that these rescuers were on their home turf, in an area where they earned a living most of the year. Still, one boat returning to St. Margarets Bay to refuel lost its bearing. Eventually, it came ashore near Lunenburg, 30 km (19 mi) as the crow flies, southwest of the crash site, and the crew walked through the woods to a house they had seen from the shore, to call for help.

When HMCS *Preserver* arrived on the scene, it took up a position slightly away from the search site. Captain Rick Town, as on-the-scene-commander, was responsible for controlling traffic through the area, both on and above the water. The *Preserver*—used during exercises and deployment to NATO missions to supply other vessels in the fleet with food, medical facilities, and fuel—also had large cold-storage lockers, which made it an excellent choice as a receiver of human remains during wartime and perhaps now, during the search for the wreck of Swissair Flight 111.

Due to the number of sea-going and airborne craft, the suspected crash zone was becoming heavily congested. Reports from Bayswater and Aspotogan indicate that, within an hour of the crash, the surrounding area was alive with small and large craft crisscrossing the water, looking for the impact site. Helicopters and aircraft were sweeping the water with their searchlights while red and amber flares drifted down from the sky, bathing the area in flickering light.

Harris and Audrey Backman live in Bayswater, about 16 km (10 mi), as the crow flies, from where Swissair 111 went down. On that night Audrey had gone to bed around 10:15 P.M. followed shortly by her husband. Harris hadn't been asleep very long when he was awakened by something, which he later assumed was the sound of the low-flying Swissair jet as it passed over his house. As he went to the kitchen for a drink of water, he heard what sounded like naval gunfire not far from shore. Naval gunfire practice was not unusual in their area, but he thought it a little strange at this time of night. Soon after, the phone rang. Audrey was surprised to hear the owner of the house next door, a CBC executive living in Ontario, on the other end of the line. She was calling to inquire as to whether they had any information on the crash of an airliner in or near St. Margarets Bay. Audrey had no sooner hung up the phone when it rang again. This time Harris answered. It was the local fire chief informing him that an airliner had crashed into St. Margarets Bay.

Harris made a quick call to RCC in Halifax, and, fortunately, was able to get through. RCC confirmed the report and told Harris they were putting out a call for six Canadian Coast Guard Auxiliary (CCGA) vessels to aid in the search. Only several weeks ago, Harris had taken over the position of operations officer for the Maritime regions of CCGA; he had been a volunteer with that organization for twenty-one years. Within a half-hour Harris and his son Steve, who lived near-by, put out to sea in Steve's 35-ft. fishing boat to begin their search between Gravel Island and White Point, the area pinpointed by RCC.

For Audrey, who had gotten out of bed when Harris had determined there was grisly work to be done at sea that night, it would be the closest she would get to a decent night's sleep in the next four days. She spent the rest of the night answering calls from around the world and manning the marine band radio in their home.

Big Tancook Island—only 6 km (4 mi) long—is located southwest of Sandy Point on the Aspotogan Peninsula and is separated from the main-land by Little Tancook Island. Both islands maintain a population of regular inhabitants, though Big Tancook boasts a greater number, about one hundred eighty. The only way out to the island is by boat; a passenger ferry runs from the mainland town of Chester.

(D. Ledger)

The wharf at Big Tancook Island from which Pastor Williams departed to search for survivors on the night of September 2, 1998.

Small as it is, Big Tancook Island has its own emergency response team. Jane Clothier, one of its members, had just gone to bed, when the sound of a jet passing came so close to her house that, for a moment, she feared the aircraft was going to go through her home. The sound of its jets faded nearly a minute later. Suddenly there was a terrific detonation, strong enough to shake her house and rattle the windows. Her grandfather, Donald Reede, who lives close by, later told her that his bedroom lit up when he heard the blast.

An hour later Ms. Clothier and many other island residents were standing, huddled against a strong easterly wind, along Big Tancook's southeastern shore. A few of them, armed with binoculars, examined the waters to the eastward looking for any signs of wreckage from the downed aircraft. Jane's husband Terry, the skipper of the Tancook Island Ferry, stood by in case the Coast Guard might require his vessel for the search.

"Flares lit up the whole [southeast] end of the island...and there were helicopters hovering around, but there wasn't much we could do because you couldn't see," she later told reporters from the *Halifax Herald*.

While those in the area of the crash wondered what they might discover, forces were at work ashore ensuring that all possible contingencies would be covered by professional personnel. Ambulances were being dispatched to the Aspotogan Peninsula from communities as far away as 200 km (125 mi). Paramedics were being recalled to work and sent to the site, with orders to bring as many medical supplies and warm blankets as they could carry. Firefighters and volunteer firefighters, armed with army surplus blankets, were amassing at fire stations all over the area, ready to lend assistance might be required. For example, in Bridgewater, about 100 km down the western shore from Halifax, more than fifty volunteer firefighters gathered, prepared for what they assumed was a land crash. Initially, they were informed that there might be as many as one hundred casualties, but that number increased as the night wore on.

At the Queen Elizabeth II Hospital in Halifax, all patients had been moved out of the Emergency Department, while all other floors had been placed on alert. Staff were being recalled to the hospital, and a triage center was set up to determine who should get first priority treatment once the number and degree of injuries were known. Four large shipments of blood were brought in, surgical teams were assembled, arrangements were made for large quantities of operating equipment, instruments, surgical gowns, bed sheets, and trolleys, ready for a flood of injured passengers. The IWK Grace Health Center and the Dartmouth General, both in the metro area, were put on an emergency footing. Hospitals and clinics along the Eastern Shore were also alerted to a possible influx of crash survivors.

As if an unseen wave of empathy were spreading throughout the fishing communities near the impact site, triggered by a history of disasters on or near the sea, fishermen and volunteers from the small coastal communities were leaving their homes and heading for the wharves where their vessels were moored. In small groups of three to five, they climbed aboard those stalwarts of the fishing fleet, the Cape Islanders. One by one they put to sea.

Pastor Phil Williams, the Baptist minister on Big Tancook Island, was asleep when the phone rang just past 10:30 P.M. The Anglican rector from a church in Chester advised him that a passenger airplane had gone down a few minutes earlier somewhere—he wasn't sure of the exact location—near Big Tancook Island. His colleague asked Williams if he would take a look around the island for any evidence of the aircraft. Williams readily agreed, thinking, God, what now?

Three months ago—to the day—the community had been rocked by a murder-suicide. An ex-patriot American employee of Department of Fisheries and Oceans arrived home from work one June day, and while his wife was at home, shot his two children and then himself. The incident, deeply affected residents of the small island community, and still weighed on the mind of Pastor Williams, a father and husband himself.

Williams dressed quickly, then climbed into his pickup and made a sweep around the island's perimeter in about five minutes. On his way home he noticed lights on at a neighbour's house; she was watching local coverage of the disaster on television. Although details were sketchy,

Williams learned that the aircraft was a Swissair passenger jet with more than one hundred people aboard.

As Williams left for home, making a sweep along the northwestern shore, he noticed several fishermen wending their way to the Government Wharf where twenty-odd boats were tied up. When he learned they were going out to look for survivors, he asked Gary Stevens, owner of the 42-ft. fishing boat *Lynette Michelle* if he could go along—a request that was willingly granted.

Williams just had time to return home to tell his wife that he was going out, and to get into some warm clothes, before the *Lynette Michelle* rounded the public wharf at 11:30 P.M. and put out to sea. Gary Stevens' brother-in-law Darren Baker, the captain of his own boat *Venture Island II*, set out at the same time, heading northeast to Hutts Point before turning south, and passing through the channel between Big and Little Tancook Islands. They turned eastward and began an hour-long trip toward the suspected impact site. Captain Stevens, Pastor Williams, and the rest of the small crew braced themselves for the worst.

Virtually within minutes of Flight 111's impact, local television stations were speculating on reports they had received on their scanners that a large aircraft had gone down in St. Margarets Bay. The RCMP and RCC were getting increasing numbers of calls not only from local press but also from international media. Within a half-hour, calls were coming in from as far away as Japan inquiring about the extent of the casualties and the nature of the crash.

For my part, by 11:00 A.M. I was watching details of the crash as they unfolded on the television in our clubhouse at Stanley Airport, an airfield located 38 kilometres northwest of Halifax International. There was speculation then about whether the Swissair flight had ditched in the ocean, and reasons for the crash were being discussed with local "experts." The first theory offered was the possibility of a bomb on board. The unresolved 1996 TWA 800 disaster of New York still loomed in everyone's mind. However, a bomb seemed less likely as reports confirmed that, even early on, the pilots had reported the smell of smoke in the cockpit. Obviously, we reasoned, an on-board fire had caused the crash. But, if that were the case, why hadn't the pilot opted to land in Yarmouth or possibly at Greenwood Air Force Base? We also wondered about the force of the impact; was the aircraft able to make a good crash landing? Our hopes for survivors were high.

Others were optimistic as well. Granville Cleveland, who had reported the sound of a crash to the Coast Guard, decided to put to sea and have a look around for himself. Though he wasn't part of the Coast Guard Auxiliary, he heard the blanket call for immediate assistance from any vessel in the area, and had called his friend Cecil Zinck, another fisherman. The two drove to the fish processing plant in New Harbour, a few kilometres south of Blandford, where Granville's 32-ft. Cape Islander *Sharon Diane* was tied up. The two of them wasted no time getting the boat ready for a trip out. Granville steered *Sharon Diane* out of New Harbour then swung southward around New Harbour Point. Once clear of the point he brought the vessel around to the east and into the teeth of a 15-knot wind, driving rain, and seas running more than a metre high. Swinging well clear of the tip of the Aspotogan Peninsula to avoid Ballast Wall Shoal, they made their way east toward the mouth of St. Margarets Bay.

While these vessels were outbound, the Coast Guard vessel *Sambro* had been busy plying the waters off Peggys Cove. Just after midnight, her searchlights picked up a fuel slick. The acrid stench of jet fuel had been in the air for more than an hour, but this was the first time the crew saw evidence on the water. Almost immediately they began running into debris—insulation, aircraft metals, and other obvious indications of an airplane crash. *Sambro* radioed her discovery to *Preserver* and gave the coordinates. One hour and fifteen minutes after the aircraft had disappeared off radar and presumably crashed, the first indications were that, if it had ditched, it had been a very hard landing.

From the beginning of the search, the area was swept by Canadian Navy equipment capable of receiving signals from Flight 111's Emergency Locator Transmitter (ELT), a device that is supposed to activate when it senses an impact greater than approximately 6 or 7 G-forces, even though it was likely that the aircraft did not have one on board because most airliners are not required to carry them. Since airliners are supposedly in constant contact with some sector of Air Traffic Control during their entire flight, ELTs aren't considered necessary.

Meanwhile, Harris Backman and his son Steve had spent some time off Gravel Island, swinging their spotlight across the water looking for any indication of a crash, when they were requested by radio from the *Preserver* to make for an area closer to Peggys Light. When they arrived on the scene an hour later, they ran into the debris field; wherever they shone the boat's light there was evidence of carnage. The debris was so thick in places that it was better to skirt around than to push through it.

Pieces of white Styrofoam, and pieces of aluminum with Styrofoam still attached keeping the metal afloat, clothing, and personal articles drifted and tossed in their searchlight. The stink of jet fuel was almost over-powering. Harris said that you could smell the site long before you reached it, particularly if you were downwind.

Despite the stench and dangerous conditions, Harris and Steve did the job they were trained to do. They picked up debris and human re-mains. From time to time they would call one of the Coast Guard cutters to come alongside and remove whatever they had pulled from the sea. Just before 5:00 a.m., Harris transferred to another boat that was going ashore so he could get some sleep before concentrating his efforts on co-ordinating his volunteers in the CCGA. His son remained for another three hours before being forced to return, slowly, to Aspotogan Harbour when his prop became fouled from some of the debris he had been steer-ing through. It took a navy diver some time to clear it, later in the day.

Harris is reluctant to talk about what he saw out on the water that night. He told me of other experiences he has had over the last twenty-one years, of towing other boats ashore, of losing a man overboard and then getting him back aboard. He talked of having a boat burn up around him and sink while at sea, and of saving another boat also on fire. He has had to put to sea to bring back a relative or friend who had died on the ocean. He will speak of those incidents, but he will not speak of what he saw at the crash site. "That's best left out there," he told me. "It was a very hard night."

Pastor Phil Williams smelled the crash site before he, skipper Gary Stevens, and the rest of the crew of *Lynette Michelle* came upon it. They had been at sea for about an hour. Stevens had been conversing with the Coast Guard and his brother-in-law on *Venture Island II*, getting vectors to the site and taking GPS fixes. About a half-hour later, guided by flares and the lights of the other vessels, they ran right into the debris field. The ob-vious devastation of the airplane surprised them all. The debris seemed to stretch away miles before them. The stench of jet fuel made Williams ill. He recalls seeing lots of insulation, but there were personal items as well. Jackets and shoes floated by the hull of *Lynette Michelle*. There were pa-pers and magazines and human remains. Over on *Venture Island II*, Skipper Darren Baker radioed the Coast Guard that he was staying close to a human torso. He did not want to bring it aboard, so they stayed by it until a vessel pulled up alongside and pulled it from the sea. Both vessels from Big Tancook Island had entertained high hopes of rescuing people. What they found instead was total devastation and evidence of severe trauma to those aboard Flight 111. Though none of these crew were part of any organized rescue team, they continued to search for survivors until 4:00 A.M. before returning disheartened to their island home.

Simultaneous to the search on the water, the crews of the Canadian Forces aircraft were flying low and slow on this less-than-ideal night for searching. Two Sea Kings out of Shearwater descended to as low as 25 m sweeping the water's surface with their searchlights, dropping flares or using night vision goggles in order to spot survivors in the heaving seas below. They had been spotting only debris since arriving on the scene. The Sea Kings were sharing airspace with an Aurora—a four-engine turbo-prop aircraft—and a twin rotor Labrador, both from 413 Rescue Squadron at CFB Greenwood.

(M. Reyno photo)

The Sea King—the much maligned over-aged workhorse of the Canadian navy's helicopter fleet.

The Aurora has electronic equipment aboard that makes it possible to scan limited areas at a time for human survivors. One piece of technology, called Forward Looking Infra-Red (FLIR), is capable of detecting tiny areas of heat radiation against an average background temperature. In other words, it could detect the heat radiating from a human body against the cold Atlantic. Because the scanning capability was limited to a small area, it was difficult to locate such a target in the vast search area. However, once a localized area of high detection probability was determined, the Aurora's crew could go to work, combing the area in a series of track crawls known as the "creeping line," or executing an expanding square search. The former is a track line that is advanced in a sort of compressed zigzag, while an expanding square search spirals outward from a point in straight lines like the sides of a box and a measured distance out from the last line on a side. With Global Positioning Satellite (GPS) navigation, this can be accomplished very accurately.

The difficulty with using a large aircraft like an Aurora is the speed at which it must fly to stay airborne. This speed, combined with the low altitude it was forced to fly due to low cloud and rain showers, made the search not only difficult but dangerous. The Labrador, like the Sea Kings, had the luxury of slow speeds and, most importantly, of hovering capability. More than a few times that night, the air search crews had hopes raised over something spotted on the water, only to be disappointed when it proved to be debris or floating clothing.

The Labrador, or Lab as they are sometimes called, has a ramp that can be lowered in the rear fuselage while in flight or while maintaining a hover, preferably the latter. It was carrying a crew of Search and Rescue technicians (SARtechs). These brave souls, clothed in dry survival suits and life vests, were prepared at a moment's notice to jump into the water in order to save a life. These rescuers can also be dispatched from the large side door of a Sea King; however, this aircraft is usually limited to training for submarine warfare and is not regularly tasked to SAR missions, which are the work of 413 Squadron in Greenwood. Circumstances arise frequently enough that these crews are tasked to rescue missions out of CFB Shearwater, due to time and distance considerations. The mission that night was a case in point, since the Swissair MD-11 crashed almost on Shearwater's doorstep, a scant thirty nautical miles away.

(M. Reyno photo)

The twin rotor Labrador helicopter has been a Search and Rescue workhorse for many years now. The crew of one such helicopter searched for survivors and wreckage after the crash. Ironically, several weeks later, that same crew perished aboard the same Labrador when it caught fire and crashed in Quebec, Canada.

The combination of types of aircraft made possible a comprehensive search of the suspected area. The searchers were using every trick in their books in an attempt to map out the area and the direction of the debris field. The helicopters dropped electronic tracking devices. These little floating buoys would drift with the debris and be tracked from space by satellites, giving the searchers invaluable clues as to the direction of the debris and a reasonable idea where it might end up in the next ten hours or so. Tide tables and weather information were fed into computers, along with the satellite information, giving a fairly accurate picture as to where the debris was heading and how fast. There was another reason for wanting a fast and accurate picture of the flow of the debris field: the possibility that a survivor might be drifting in it. Knowing where the debris was, where it had been, and where it might be in an hour would give the searchers a chance to get to an area quickly, thereby saving precious minutes in a search for someone who might be succumbing to hypothermia.

Like everyone involved in the search for survivors, the crews of the military rescue contingent were soon disappointed. Capt. Nancy Taber, navigator aboard one of the Sea Kings, told reporter Christine Doucet from the *Halifax Herald*, "We didn't see very much out there—a bunch of little pieces of what looked to be blue foam, white foam, black foam—a lot of stuff that we couldn't determine what it was." Captain Taber also noted that there was a lot of fuel out in the search area. The stench of jet fuel became a signature of the wreck site. For the rescuers, it would be associated forever with the stench of death.

The Canadian Navy, RCMP vessels (Zodiacs), and the Coast Guard were serving as deposit sites for the debris, human remains, and personal effects pulled from the water that night. Perhaps their jobs were the toughest of all. The Zodiacs and smaller Coast Guard vessels were responsible for locating and off-loading the material and remains found by the fishing and pleasure boats. They would transport this cargo to the naval vessels *Ville de Quebec* and *Preserver*.

HMCS *Preserver* was probably the most-affected vessel of the flotilla. Her cold-storage lockers were used to preserve the remains of passengers and crew of Flight 111. *Preserver*'s crew had the unenviable task of receiving the human remains, cataloguing them, bagging them, then placing them in lockers for later disbursement to the coroner ashore.

Preserver's captain, Rick Town, had a crew of nearly three hundred, including some RCMP personnel aboard his ship that night. By 3:30 A.M. on Thursday it was obvious to them that there was little hope of any survivors. Pieces of debris were coming aboard at an ever-increasing rate, and so were the human remains—*Preserver*'s top priority, which personnel aboard the supply ship were processing as quickly as they could, putting them in body bags, which were then taken aboard Sea Kings that landed on *Preserver*'s helicopter pad.

At 3:50 A.M. on September 3, the first body and the *only* intact body to be recovered—a woman—was lifted from an RCMP vessel to the dock at

Peggys Cove. Reports of partial remains were coming in, depleting all hope for survivors. This was disheartening for everyone involved. That night the padre aboard *Preserver* had his hands full dealing with not only his own anguish and bitter disappointment, but also that of the crew.

The other Canadian naval vessel operating near the crash scene, *Ville de Québec*, one of Canada's newest and fastest frigates, had steamed to the site from 35 nautical miles to the southwest. She was on site in just over an hour of receiving a call from RCC for assistance. The new Halifax Class frigates are very maneuverable, which is why the *Ville de Québec* was tasked to this area. At about 3:00 A.M. she ran across the debris field, but *Ville de Québec*'s crew and captain, Cmdr. Sylvain Allaire, were frustrated in their attempts to find the actual centre of the crash site because of heavy seas and the combination of driving rain, wind, and tide. Some time later the frigate came across human remains, and the crew were disturbed by the condition of what they did find; their judgement of what had befallen the aircraft changed. *Ville de Québec* would spend two more days and nights sweeping the waters before being relieved and sent back to safe harbour.

"Obviously it affects the way you think and the way you react," Commander Allaire told reporters at the *Daily News*, but morale was good; the team aspect improves, if that makes sense. Time will tell, I guess, how it affects everyone individually."

Out on the water, there were brief moments of hope when the would-be rescuers thought they had found someone alive. Maj. Michel Brisebois at RCC had informed the press at one point that an inflated life raft had been found. Upon closer investigation, however, it was determined that the raft, which was badly torn, had self-inflated and the damage to it probably was caused by the impact.

Derek Levy, another fishing boat operator from Blandford, had a similar experience. He had been out all night in miserable weather. While looking for survivors, his hopes and the hopes of his crew were temporarily lifted by the sight of two semi-inflated life rafts. They maneuvered carefully toward the rafts, but their spirits were soon dashed when they realized both rafts held only sea water. For that brief moment, there had been a slight chance that someone from the hapless airliner was still alive. They returned to the search, playing their spotlight across the heaving waters, their vision hampered by the rain lancing through its beam. Nevertheless, it was becoming apparent to everyone out on the water that there were going to be no last-minute rescues, no happy stories.

Lines of traffic, particularly during the tourist season, are a common sight at Peggys Cove and the area around the Sou'wester Restaurant. The lighthouse at Peggys Cove has adorned postcards for decades and, along with pictures of the Cabot Trail in Cape Breton, has signified the so-called heart of Nova Scotia. The type of traffic on this night was not usually seen in such numbers. Dozens of ambulances lined the road into the tiny village. Fire trucks, military transports, Red Cross vans, police cruisers, and other rescue vehicles choked the parking lot behind the restaurant. Meanwhile, another contingent pushed its way in—the media. At an astonishing rate, local media was being augmented by line press reporters, freelance journalists, and stringers, the forerunners of the heavyweight television networks from around the world and reporters from the major daily newspapers. In the space of an hour, the Swissair crash was to become the top news story around the world.

By 2:30 A.M. reports were indicating little in the way of "rumoured survivors." Between 3:30 and 4:00 A.M. messages began going out to the local hospitals and to ambulance operators. Their services would no longer be required. Hospitals were told to stand down and the number of ambulances was trimmed to very few. The unofficial word was beginning to spread: there was little likelihood of any survivors.

For Morris Green, a spokesman for Nova Scotia's Emergency Health Services, this was depressing news. He had fourteen ambulances posted along the South Shore within twenty minutes of a call from the RCMP. Other ambulances from the greater Halifax metro area and as far away as Digby were on alert with thirty of their attendant paramedics.

"There were a lot of paramedics that were in a pretty grim mood by the middle of the morning when they found out there wouldn't be any survivors," Green said.

Early on, empty ambulances had waited in lines at local fire halls, and in some of the smaller communities along the western side of the Aspotogan Peninsula, notably in Blandford and Bayswater. Volunteer firefighters were grouped at an abandoned work site, a nearly-completed private health complex called the Sea Spa further to the east on Highway 329. When word came through that the crash site was closer to Peggys Cove than Bayswater and Blandford, there was a mass exodus of ambulances, fire trucks, police cruisers, and personnel from the Aspotogan Peninsula to Peggys Cove, about a 60-km (31 mi) trip around St. Margarets Bay. As it turned out, they would never be needed.

At approximately 5:00 A.M. the sun burst over the eastern horizon and illuminated the seas off Peggys Cove to reveal the horrific scene that the flares and spotlights had only hinted at. The radios aboard the boats out on the water, which until then had been busy with chatter, abruptly went silent. The rescuers were suddenly confronted by the enormity of the catastrophe that must have overtaken Swissair Flight 111.

The Day Search

Despite the fact that there was little hope now of finding any survivors, the dedication of government and civilian rescuers did not falter. Some of those who had been out the evening before on their fishing and pleasure boats, and had gone ashore for a few hours of sleep, now returned to help look for and recover debris and remains.

For their part, the military personnel manning the warships and the crews of the Coast Guard vessels, the crews on RCMP Zodiacs, and the Fisheries vessels were beginning to show the strain of their work. While smaller boats were dealing with body parts one at a time, the crews of the these larger ships and vessels were dealing with an influx of findings from about sixty men, women, and children.

Maj. Denis Lajeunesse, the acting commander of 413 Search and Rescue Squadron in Greenwood, told the press that the original idea was to pick up survivors and transport them to Shearwater, but "it quickly became obvious that this was a search for debris and the retrieval of bodies."

The transporting of human remains from the *Preserver* and *Ville de Quebec* fell to the Sea Kings, which had been out searching all night. Because they were capable of landing on the helipads of both *Preserver* and *Ville de Quebec*, they were re-tasked from search and rescue to aerial hearses. Remains were being evacuated to CFB Shearwater, across the harbour from the city of Halifax, to a hangar designated as a temporary morgue, staffed at the outset by some twenty pathologists, doctors, and dentists.

One Sea King crew member, Maj. Donald LeBlanc, reflected the thoughts of many of the professional crews when he noted that you had to keep your feelings in check in cases like this. They had a job to do and had to steel themselves to it, as they had on many other occasions. They hoped for the best but were often disappointed.

Military and civilian agencies carry out as many as two thousand missions each year in Eastern Canada alone, some of them more successful than others. The highly skilled and trained military contingent often risk their lives and are not strangers to sudden death on the Atlantic.

Over the next few days, the ship's crew and the RCMP officers aboard *Preserver* would bear the brunt of managing human remains from the crash site, which took an emotional toll on everyone. Capt. Rick Town described the operation as gruesome but vital. He and the crew simply braced themselves as they not only had to handle the human remains—some obviously from children and teenagers—but also personal items. Teddy bears, toys, photographs, handwritten letters, and articles of clothing brought home the fact that, only hours before, these items were in the hands of their owners, items so similar to those that the crew's own loved ones had at home. Everything was so familiar in such an unlikely and ghastly setting.

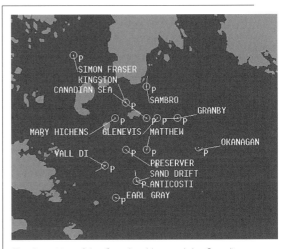

The disposition of the Canadian Navy and the Canadian Coast Guard's assets on September 5.

By mid-morning of September 3, the searchers were running out of body bags. Fshermen resorted to using plastic bags to hold remains until they could pass them along to a Coast Guard or naval vessel. The number of boats out on the water had expanded to such a point that the On-Scene-Commander, Capt. Rick Town, had to start restricting access to the debris field in order to prevent debris from sinking or from incurring further damage by propellor action.

At 11:00 A.M. the navy and SAR officials held a press conference in Halifax, where they suggested it was still early enough in the search that they were holding out hope for survivors, in spite of discouraging evidence to the contrary. Though it was still too early for dive teams to attempt a recovery of black boxes (or any other submerged wreckage) two minesweepers were dispatched, knowledgeable of the area, positioning themselves for the underwater task.

Granville Cleveland returned to the debris field with Kevin Mountain, another crew member, on *Sharon Diane* despite his misgivings. He had returned to New Harbour at about 4:00 A.M. after a night of searching, which he described as one of his most disturbing experiences. He did what he could to get some sleep before heading back out on the water by noon of the same day. This time, though, he had a newspaper reporter aboard, Mike Harris from the *Toronto Sun*.

Sharon Diane was plying the waters off East Ironbound Island, about 9 km southwest of the estimated crash site, when it ran into debris. Wherever it had impacted, the debris and human remains were being influenced by tidal action and winds to drift to the west, toward the tip of the Aspotogan Peninsula, East Ironbound Island, Big and Little Tancook Islands, and further westward into Mahone Bay. Once into Mahone Bay there were plenty of little islands and rocks for debris to fetch up on, which eventually would create a major problem for the searchers. These areas, and to some extent other areas to the south and north, would require a month of searching by Canadian Army personnel and dedicated volunteers from Nova Scotia's well-trained ground SAR teams.

For now, Granville Cleveland, Kevin Mountain, and Mike Harris sailed through the fragmented occupants and airframe of Flight 111. They rolled through seas running up to nearly 2 m (6 ft.). Kevin and Mike used boat hooks to snag personal effects and remains as they slid by the hull of the Cape Islander. Granville was manning the wheel and keeping a sharp eye forward, making sure he didn't run over anything that might be important. In particular he didn't want to run afoul of any poor souls in the water.

A sudden thought had occurred to him while he was out on the water that afternoon. Normally he would be setting out his nets here to catch mackerel, what he used as bait in his lobster traps. He told Mike Harris he didn't think that he would be setting nets out on Mahone Bay for a long time, not with what might still be out there waiting to be caught.

When I asked Granville Cleveland what it had been like that night and day, he really didn't want to talk about it. He did say that, though they had come across many human remains, they didn't bring them aboard the vessel. They were more comfortable with keeping them alongside and calling one of the RCMP or Coast Guard Zodiacs to deal with them.

Kevin Mountain was no stranger to things gory. He was a former member of the Canadian Armed Forces and had seen his share of human tragedy. During one operation, he had been in a demolition accident. Personnel had been exposed to an explosion, but he admitted that the result was nothing like what he had seen out there on the water.

Like Granville Cleveland and Kevin Mountain, many who had been out the night before were out again the next day, continuing their search. But it was beginning to tell on them. After the sight of so many headless torsos and severed limbs, and in one case the long hair of a young woman on a faceless head, some fishermen began to quit and head to shore. These were not faint-hearted people. The faint-hearted don't make a living fishing in small boats on the North Atlantic. These were people who had reached the limit of how much they could endure. But for most of them, returning home did not erase the memories of that night; it will take years for those to fade.

On shore during September 3, Audrey Backman, who had spent the previous night manning the radio and answering the phone, was asked a few times to pick up fishermen who had come ashore in a port other than their own because they had been low on fuel or were exhausted. She would drive them back to their homes, where they made arrangements to get their vessels back to their own harbour.

On the drive home, the fishermen often talked about what they had seen out there, horrendous details she would have preferred not to hear. But she let them talk because she knew they had to give voice to the unimaginable carnage they had witnessed. Audrey could take solace only in that she did not have to witness first-hand what they had. She was working on her second day without sleep. She had nearly two more to go.

Although some boats called off the search, there were still many out on the water after midday. Many boats were carrying members of the media from around the world. They, too, were touched and affected by this tragedy. For the most part, they refrained from showing the gore out on the water. Mike Harris of the *Toronto Sun* may have stated the case for all of them when he opened his report from Ironbound Island on that day by writing, "The faceless head, its long, honey-blonde hair fanning out on the silvery sea, announced the horror of what had happened to Swissair Flight 111 as well as anything."

Jimmy Mayo, captain of the charter boat *Peggy's Light*, had been talking with some of his friends who had been out on the water the night before, searching for survivors. The RCMP had him on standby since dawn that day. He was in no hurry now to get to sea. "From what I've heard from them," he said, "I'd rather stay on land than go out there."

Phil Chatterton, a private pilot, would normally have gone to work that day, but when the early-morning call came via RCC to the volunteer organization that he belonged to asking him to standby, he did. His services might be required because the crews flying the early morning of September 3 had been rotated back to base to get rested for their next trip out. Phil, now the Zone Commander for the Halifax zone, was a trained search pilot with the Civil Air Search and Rescue Association (CASARA), a nationwide volunteer organization dedicated to searching for lost hunters, hikers, children, even downed aircraft. For the most part, CASARA use their own aircraft for these searches, usually a four-seater with a pilot, navigator, and two spotters in the back. Usually their activities are restricted to land searches and coastal crawling, with the occasional search just off the shoreline a few hundred metres. Sometimes their volunteers are called on by the CAF to double as spotters on their aircraft, when they're short-handed. This was the case on September 3.

Chatterton waited through the night, anticipating a phone call that would activate him to search status. When he had heard nothing by morning, he prepared for work. A few minutes before 7:00 A.M. the call came from Dave McMahone, himself a spotter, asking him to report to CFB Shearwater straight away. For Chatterton this was a short trip, since he lived scarcely a mile away. He ran back into the house and changed out of his suit into something more appropriate to the task.

When he arrived at the base, two of the three civilian spotters were waiting for him. A few minutes later the fourth member arrived, asking where was the Herc to take them out. Chatterton pointed to the sky, indicating a C-130 on final approach for the base. The aircraft pulled onto the Tarmac and swung to face the taxiway; its rear ramp dropped, and the four spotters hung onto their hats as they ran against the prop blast into the aircraft's interior. They received a quick briefing while the C-130 taxied back to the runway. Shortly after 8:00 A.M. they were airborne, en route to the crash site.

Spotters on an aircraft are seated at a window on either side of the plane and are given instructions as to what they are looking for, usually, as in this case, in a pre-briefing before takeoff. They are supplied with a headset with a boom microphone attached, which is plugged into the aircraft's intercom system. This puts them in direct communication with the pilot. Should the spotter see something of interest to the search, he advises the pilot on which side of the aircraft the sighting has occurred and the direction the pilot should turn to locate the subject and have it verified by the pilot or navigator.

Travelling in the back of a rumbling C-130 "Herc," Labrador helicopter, or even a private plane can be extremely tiring over extended periods of time. The constant turning / banking, climbing and descending, the vibration of the aircraft, the Spartan conditions which bear little resemblance to airliners, and the smell of fuel on a Hercules all wear a person down and make the novice nauseous. And a Hercules, with its long fuel endurance, can stay aloft for as long as ten hours before returning to base for fuel and a fresh crew.

(M. Reyno photo)

Three C-130 Hercules similar to that on which Phil Chatterton acted as a civilian CASARA spotter, searching for debris and bodies off Peggys Cove on September 3.

Chatterton, like the other spotters with the Halifax Zone of Nova Scotia's CASARA—Dave McMahone, Don MacLeod, and Mike Doiron—was uncertain what he might see as they flew out toward the Atlantic. He knew about the crash of the Swissair airliner but knew little of the details concerning the extent of damage.

Upon its arrival on site, the Herc was tasked by the on-scene-commander to search the suspected outer limits of the debris field for anything that might have drifted that far due to winds, waves, and tidal action. The task would be much easier for the Hercules from its vantage point than for the dozens of small vessels.

From altitudes of 600 to 700 ft., the C-130's course defined the outlines of the search field. From time to time they would spot something and the Herc's pilot would take the aircraft down to 300 ft. for a closer look. Like everyone who had been searching the waters for the last ten hours, they were slowly coming to the realization that they were not going to find survivors. As they closed in from the perimeter and crossed into denser areas of debris, the sheer volume of material floating on the water attested to what must have been the near-total destruction of the Boeing MD-11. For several kilometres, mostly white Styrofoam insulation spread out before them, with wakes cut through it by the search vessels.

Once the spotters noted a bubbling or roiling in the water which, from their altitude, could have been a shoal or gases escaping from something below. They dispatched a helicopter to check out the anomaly and were told that it was a shoal just below the surface.

An Aurora was also tracking across the debris field, sharing the same airspace 200 ft. below them. It had activated its Magnetic Anomaly Detection (MAD) boom, the appendage that sticks out of its tail like a stinger, in an attempt to pick some aircraft parts out of the confusing mess. Eventually the crew gave up, because they had so many hits that it was impossible to track them all.

About one hour after midday, the Dutch-American cruise ship *Veen Dam* was leaving the area. Her crew had provided around-the-clock assistance since early that morning, when she had steamed to the area after picking up the Coast Guard's call to any ships in the area for assistance. Fully loaded with passengers, it spent most of the time keeping station over the believed position of Flight 111's impact site. Captain Town expressed his gratitude to *Veen Dam*'s crew and officers as they were leaving.

Veen Dam's captain responded, "It's our pleasure, sir. Sorry we couldn't do more."

From an altitude of 600 ft. it was easy to look at the field of destruction below, be impressed with its size, yet still feel detached from it. Phil Chatterton experienced this detachment to some degree but described how, at one point, the human side of the disaster was brought home. Amidst the flotsam and jetsam—chair backs, life vests, Styrofoam and bits of floating metal—was a pair of light blue pants floating V-shaped on the surface, as if they had been laid out on a bed for wearing. They made two passes over the trousers, making sure they were not a body or a part of one.

Mike Doiron is the Regional Aviation Safety Officer (Maritimes) for Transport Canada and serves as the Halifax Zone's CASARA Safety Officer. Doiron remembers the experience as surreal. Time seemed to stand still. He remembers the light blue trousers, too, and a bright yellow jacket among the debris.

Part of the standard procedure for spotting is a twenty-minute turn at the window, then off for twenty. The eyes tire easily from the method used for visual detecting, called scanning, which increases the chances of spotting something on the water or ground due to the eye's acuity. Doiron noted that after only three turns at the window, he was getting very tired, which he assumed had something to do with the urgency of the situation and the spotter's natural determination to see something that might be important or that might save a life.

The Hercules returned to base at about 5:00 P.M. but landed this time at Greenwood. An hour later, with a fresh flight crew aboard, the C-130 took off and returned the CASARA spotters to their home base at CFB Shearwater. When the spotters deplaned they saw a new set of passengers ready to come aboard, not to search this time but to see. These passengers included Flavio Cotti, President of the Swiss Confederation, and Jeffrey Katz, the Swissair CEO, along with some of Swissair's executives. Before leaving, the spotters were thanked by the C-130's flight crew for their efforts. Like the captain of *Van Deem*, the spotters only wished they could have done more.

By the evening of September 3—not yet twenty-four hours since the crash—Major Michel Brisebois of RCC was possibly one of the few officials involved in the search who had not given up hope that someone might be found alive. Even Swissair had, that afternoon, issued a statement that it was clear none of the 229 passengers and crew of Flight 111 had survived. But Major Brisebois was aware of studies done by the Canadian Navy off these very shores, indicating that, at this time of the year, a large healthy male could survive in these waters for up to thirty-six hours. Curiously the water is warmest in September and October on the east coast of Nova Scotia, warmed by its land mass and the influence of the Gulf Stream. Just then the water temperatures inshore were averaging 16°C (approximately 64°F). As far as Major Brisebois was concerned, there was still a chance, and even if there was only one survivor, the whole search would be worth it. Hypothermia was the enemy, the passing of time its agent. The length of time a body could tolerate the slow sapping of heat is dependent on body mass and the amount of fat, a good insulator from cold. The thinner the person, the more susceptible they would be to hypothermia.

There was always the possibility that one or more survivors had drifted westerly into Mahone Bay, a natural catchment area of warmer waters. There are hundreds of little islands, coves, harbours, even rocks where a person could have drifted and been hidden. Until they were satisfied that this was not the case and the maximum survival time from hypothermia had not passed, the officials directing the operation were not going to advise the media that they had given up hope of finding survivors.

The media, for their part, had turned the Swissair crash into worldwide news. The American press rolled into the tiny village of Peggys Cove with a single-minded purpose. It wasn't long before they were flashing American dollars, which at the time were worth one-third more than their

Canadian counterpart. There were stories of a TV satellite truck that backed into a resident's holding tank, damaging it. On the spot the home owner was given $5,000 U.S. for the damage, then the TV crew proceeded to rent the house for $1,000 U.S. per day. In Halifax, when the vehicle rental agencies' supply of cars and trucks dried up, one American network purchased six new Lincolns to accommodate their needs.

Some fishermen experienced this boon as well. Many media personnel were taken out to the site that first night and early the next day by the fishermen; however, some were put off by the manner and behaviour of their passengers and returned them to shore and gave them back their money. In other instances, both fishermen and the media were turned away from the perimeters of the search site by Canadian Coast Guard and Fisheries and Oceans vessels. Their persistence was so relentless at the command centre set up at Peggys Cove that reporters were told if they did not cease and desist they would be arrested and detained if they attempted to cross into the perimeter.

Perhaps the greatest immediate impact the media had on the local situation was the log jam created on telecommunications networks. The local telephone company, experienced a near breakdown in communications links and had to recall all of their personnel and create new links. The cellular phone network and its system of towers had to be augmented in order to carry the increased of cellular traffic.

Overnight, the population of Peggys Cove had risen from sixty to nearly a thousand. The roads were jammed with vehicles. An antenna forest sprung up not far from the media centre at the Sou'wester Restaurant, which had been taken over as the main press conference site for the dissemination of press reports from the military, the police, and the forensic pathology communications people. Later on forensic reports would be released from CFB Shearwater, but for several days the hard-pressed restaurant bore the brunt of the media influx until the whole operation was moved to the World Trade and Convention Centre in Halifax.

Many local residents and fishermen experienced their fifteen minutes of fame when the media, desperate for anything to fill the information gap, interviewed them, asking for their feelings and their input on what might be expected out there on the water. What was it like out there? What did you see? Did you pick up any body parts or any personal effects? To some of these questions they would respond, but it has been my experience, even eight months later, that many of the people who went out that night and the following day really did not want to talk about the grisly recovery operation.

These hardy people have their own way of coping that likely stems from living day by day with the possibility of sudden death, and their strong sense of community and empathy with those who die at sea. For many of them, this was not the first time they had to pull bodies, strangers on this occasion, from the Atlantic. But there was a difference. This time what they dredged from the waters was not always identifiable as human. So when Pastor Williams, Granville Cleveland, Harris and Steve Backman, Phil Chatterton, Mike Doiron, and so many others returned to their beds on the night of September 3, perhaps twenty-four hours after the crash, whatever satisfaction they may have had from responding to the call for help was obscured by a sense of failure: they had searched for survivors, hoping to restore them to their families safe and sound, and had found none.

CHAPTER THREE

Diving into a
"House of Horrors"

When I was four years old, I stood with my father on a wharf at the edge of the Mira River, a beautiful semi-saltwater inlet on northeastern Cape Breton Island. While he was talking with the owner of the wharf, I jumped—without warning and fully clothed—into the water. To this day I can remember sitting on the bottom, eyes open, watching seaweed fronds wave back and forth. My father promptly extricated me from my view of the Mira by grabbing my hair and returning me to my former position on the wharf.

I have never harboured any fear of the water. Rather I've had considerable fascination with it. I eventually learned to swim, using a cheap face mask to see underwater. I graduated to the surface while living near a canal just outside Dartmouth. I grew up around the water so it was probably inevitable that I would become a sport scuba diver in my late teens. And I once had a short stint working as a diver while in between jobs. My experience gives me some knowledge of the profession and the difficulties divers encounter, particularly in the cold and unforgiving waters off Canada's eastern coast.

When Flight 111 crashed off Peggys Cove, there were immediate attempts to pinpoint the location of the impact site, which did not come to light for ten hours into the search. Discovering the reasons for a passenger airliner crash is an urgent matter, in order to determine if other air carriers might be at risk. Everyone wants the problem identified and fixed immediately or, failing that, the other aircraft grounded until the problem is addressed.

The mutual hope of searchers, investigators, and media was to locate not only survivors of Flight 111 but also to retrive the aircraft's black boxes—

the Flight Data Recorder (FDR) and the Cockpit Voice Recorder (CVR)—to throw some light on what might have caused the crash. Both pieces of equipment were believed to be fixed with a "pinger" that would help in locating them, if they weren't too severely damaged. Damage was a real fear, for, if initial observations by the searchers of the debris field were any indication, the destruction of the MD-11 must have been near total, which is almost unheard of. Because there seemed to be no signals coming from the CVR and FDR, HMCS *Okanagan*—an Oberan Class Canadian submarine purchased by Canada from the British in 1967 and due to be decommissioned within days of the disaster—would be pressed into service to locate by sonar the pingers on the black boxes. The *Okanagan* was rewarded with the discovery of one if not two pingers on Friday, September 4.

Before any diving could begin, the actual site of the Flight 111 wreck had to be found. A side-scan sonar fish was towed behind one of the naval ships until the main wreckage site was discovered. Some early search data did seem to suggest that fairly large portions of the aircraft's fuselage were still intact on the bottom; however, this would prove false within a couple of weeks—most likely what had been detected was an underwater reef. The new coastal defence vessels HMCS *Kingston* and HMCS *Anticosti* crisscrossed the area of the debris field in an attempt to map the total wreckage site using bottom and side-scanning sonar. Although they had not discovered anything on the bottom to indicate large pieces of wreckage, the searchers believed that they just had not discovered it yet. The largest pieces they were finding were not much more than a metre square.

(DND photo)

HMCS Okanagan, *the submarine used to locate the "pingers" on the FDR and CVR and the location of the actual impact site of Fl-111.*

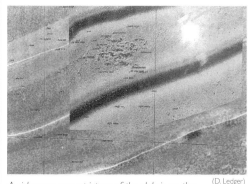

(D. Ledger)

A side-scan sonar picture of the debris on the bottom. The dark shadowy lines are the tracks of the sonar where it doesn't see what is directly below itself.

The eighty Canadian divers, who would be working in pairs were assisted by thirty-six American divers from USS *Grapple*, a United States Navy vessel specifically designed to recover heavy loads from the sea bottom. This same vessel had been instrumental in the recovery sections of the TWA Flight 800 Boeing 747 that had crashed off New York in 1996. And it would be asked again to participate in the recovery of the wreck of Egyptair Flight 990 from the Atlantic off Martha's Vineyard, another flight which originated out of New York, thirteen months after the Swissair crash. The sophisticated laser-scanning equipment of USS *Grapple* eventually determined that the supposed large sections of the MD-11 were in fact large piles of smaller debris. The Grapple launched a Deep Drone that was capable of mapping out the debris field. Once this had been completed, a salvage plan was drawn up in order to better focus the search. In the meantime, the Canadian Coast Guard cutter *Hudson* was outfitted with the U.S. Navy laser scanner and was getting very high-resolution pictures of the bottom, images that far exceeded those of the side-scan sonar.

(DND photo)
Two U.S. Navy divers from the USN Grapple *are lowered to the bottom, diving on the main wreckage of Flight 111, which lay in 185 feet of water. On this descent their task was to recover bodies.*

At this stage, the Transportation Safety Board (TSB) and Canadian Navy needed to focus their efforts on retrieving as many human remains as possible. Had they recklessly torn the debris apart, human body parts vital to the forensic identification team led by Dr. John Butt, Nova Scotia's chief medical examiner, might have been further damaged or lost, making a difficult job even worse. As it was, the near-freezing water temperatures were helping to preserve the human flesh and organs. Another consideration was the possibility that some remains would be intact, a condition the relatives of the victims hoped for, and a definite help to Dr. Butt's team: an intact body might explain conditions in the passenger cabin that night. However, subsequent work by the divers made it clear that there were not going to be any intact remains recovered from the ocean floor. The devastation was too great, the G-forces too high, and the human body too frail to survive such an impact at such a high speed, which was estimated at 1000-1140 kph (600-700 mph).

It was known early on that most of the wreckage was in deep water—preliminary indications suggested the depth would be between 30 and 57 m (100 and 190 ft). Because the exact location of the main body of the aircraft—assuming there was one—was initially uncertain, the investigative body of the TSB, the navy, and the Coast Guard was loath to commit divers unnecessarily to a search. They decided to wait until the surface search had run its course. In any event, Navy Clearance Divers from the Fleet Diving Unit at Shearwater, mobilized fairly early in the search, would not be able to get their vessels *Granby* and *Sechelt* on site for another day and a half following the crash. The *Granby* arrived on scene the morning of September 4 and the *Sechelt* arrived the next day.

(DND photo)

The USN Grapple *moored and prepared to lift heavy debris from the ocean floor. It was originally thought that large portions of Flight 111 were still intact on the bottom.*

As difficult as the task would be, divers had exhaustive training, skill, and determination to do the job, which would serve them well during Operation Persistence. The recovery of human remains and the discovery of the black boxes—in that order—were their primary objectives. They were also given instructions to keep an eye out for components from the

(D. Ledger)

The Granby, one of two Canadian navy dive tenders responsible for the positioning, deploying, and recovering of divers on the wreck site.

(DND photo)

The Sechelt, working with the Granby, deployed and recovered divers off Peggys Cove during the first month of Operation Persistance.

MD-11's electronic equipment bay and flight deck.

The investigators were looking for data processing equipment that might house what are known as "non-volatile" computer memory chips. These are chips that continue to store data in their memory circuits even though no power is flowing through them. They could be rewired into the circuitry of another identical piece of equipment and the information downloaded. The TSB was also looking for burnt wiring or any other burnt items from the cockpit area.

Once the location of the main wreckage was generally established and the acoustic pingers were roughly located within a more manageable area, divers set to work from the Granby and Sechelt. The navy divers, most of them Clearance Divers from the Canadian Navy's Fleet Diving Unit, were in the water only two days after the crash, on the afternoon of September 4. For most of them this would be their first encounter with such a terrible wreck. For many it would be akin to a nightmare better suited to a grisly movie. They began their underwater search using hand-held locators to recover the black boxes. After an aircraft crash, the retrieval of the black box is always the first priority in case whatever caused that crash could cause another airplane to do the same. The portable sonar units, limited in their useful range, were of greater value once the search area had been pinpointed. Another problem with these devices was the reflectivity of the metal hiding the black box pingers, which could scatter the signal, making it difficult to localize. They made three dives that first day, with one pair of divers down at a time. The divers felt they were making progress, despite a limited visibility of only 5 m (16 ft). However, they had to postpone operations due to the weather. The next day they were back in the water.

Because it was obvious that body and debris recovery was going to be a major effort, divers worked from stages lowered to the bottom by the dive tenders. The stage is a rectangular aluminum platform with grills on the two ends and a cross piece on top, to which the winch cable is attached. In front of and behind the divers, slightly above waist level, are two rails with which they can steady themselves. On either side and slightly below the cage are two concrete clumps used to counter the stage's natural tendency to swing at the end of a long line, and to keep the stage in place once it is on the bottom.

During the dive operation it would only make sense to have divers on an umbilical system, meaning the diver is connected to the surface by an umbilical hose attached to a full face mask, an unlimited supply of air, and voice communications. The umbilical cord joining the diver to the surface served more than one purpose. It not only supplied a mixture of oxygen and helium but also hot water through a separate hose, which heated the dry suit. Thick communications lines were threaded in with the hoses, as well as a video cable, and a power cable that supplied voltage for the helmet light. Bundled together, these cables are as big around as a man's wrist and are covered in a Gore-Tex or Kevlar layer for protection from damage. The umbilical line is strong enough to pull up a diver from the depths.

Once the topside crew and the suited-up divers were satisfied that everything appeared in working order, the divers were walked onto the stage and carefully lifted from the deck of the tender, swung out over the side, and lowered into the water. They were submerged a few metres into the water and then held while some checks were made for suit leaks, power shorts to the lights, and to ensure that the communication lines were working. Once the dive team was assured that everything was in good working order, the descent continued.

Trips to the bottom were accomplished quickly but cautiously. Once on the bottom, the divers advised that they were exiting the stage. They had to bend forward and walk backwards under the horizontal bar, off the stage, and onto the bottom. The reason for this little manoeuvre was to ensure that the umbilical lines would be routed through this stage structure. Once away from the stage, divers would have the umbilical line to follow back to the structure should there be a problem with disorientation or poor visibility. Even though there was good visibility on this operation, the divers could see to distances of only 6 to 7.5 m.

Safety checks were made before leaving the area of the stage, and then the careful scan of the bottom began. Navy divers working on the Swissair wreck site quickly discovered that walking on the metal debris was hazardous. The brass bottom of their boots caused metal to metal slippage. In an environment already fraught with danger, slipping on razor-sharp metal was unacceptable. So a relatively new boot on the market was used instead one with a hard, thick, rubber bottom, one with heavily weighted to keep the diver's centre of gravity low. These and other weights strapped on the divers afforded them an upright posture and kept them firmly planted on the bottom.

The debris these divers had to search and constantly move through was hazardous. During one press conference, Commander Greg Aikins, who at the time was commanding officer for the search operation at HMCS *Halifax*, likened the scene on the bottom to a "house of horrors."

"The impact was catastrophic," stated Commander Aikins in a ship-to-shore interview with *Halifax Herald* staff reporter Susan LeBlanc. "Clearly, we have not seen [intact bodies] so far." He also described the dangerous conditions that existed below. "It's like walking through a giant pile of razor blades. But safety has been our number one priority."

(DND photo)

A Canadian diver in full "kit" prepares to descend to the site. The heavy multi-purpose cable at his feet carries hot water to heat his suit, along with a video cable, a microphone cable, an air supply, and electrical power for the light mounted on the left side of his helmet. His outer garment is a dry-suit with a heavy undergarment. He wears heavily weighted, corrugated rubber- and metal-soled boots, which provide traction, keep him upright underwater, and protect his feet from hazardous, razor-sharp metal.

The divers had to stand in the debris to gain the necessary leverage needed to lift a piece of the aircraft away from a body section pinned below it. Pieces of human remains were skewered by metals or sandwiched between layers of metal or plastic and had to be pulled free. Often body fluids not yet disturbed formed a cloud in front of the divers, or tendrils of flesh not yet consumed by sea life detached and drifted around them. The ever-present Styrofoam insulation would flutter upward unexpectedly. Caught out of the corner of the eye or popping straight into the diver's mask, it could cause the diver to lose his balance and grab for something to stabilize himself that was sharp or ragged-edged. A house of horrors, indeed. Mercifully, the divers were rotated through their shifts, having only about a half-hour down before they were recovered and shepherded into the recompression chamber, nursing a cup of coffee and their own dark thoughts for the next few hours.

The handlers above had to pay out as much umbilical as possible without letting it drag through the wreckage on the bottom or pull the divers off their feet. A de-scrambler electronically enhanced the divers' voices, drenched in helium gas and affected by the cold water and pressure, to make their voices more readable for communications. Their voices still sounded unnatural, something like a 45 record playing at 33 RPM. Gases were carefully metered down to the divers and times were carefully monitored. Those personnel not concerned with immediate diver attention watched on video monitors as divers picked up pieces of "those not now living," as one diver referred to the human remains, piled wreckage into baskets lowered from the tenders, or hooked nylon line to the larger pieces for hoisting by winch to the surface.

Weather during the early search was foul, and the sea state, even when the weather cleared, was only slightly improved. Because the edges of Hurricane Danielle had just passed through the area, waves were still running up to 2 m (6.5 ft) and were close together and steep, rather than long, rolling swells. Diving in this type of sea is possible but also dangerous, with the topside support. The constant tossing of boats and divers can result in injuries from divers smashing against a hull. There is always the danger of a valve fitting on a compressed air tank getting fractured or, worse still, the tank getting punctured and exploding like a bomb. The latter was unlikely to happen during the dive off Peggys Cove due to the use of different equipment. In the search for Flight 111, the navy divers were in still greater danger because of the depth at which the wreckage lay—nearly 61 m (200 ft).

The particular conditions underwater would make the divers' work more difficult. Deep wave action can reach well below the surface, hampering the diver, causing weariness and loss of sound judgement. It becomes extremely dangerous when a diver is tossed about in an area of large, jagged, razor-sharp pieces of metal. At the necessary depth, every inch of the diver's body would be subjected to five and half times more pressure than we are used to on the surface.

Poor visibility also posed serious obstacles to the divers. To mitigate the expected difficult conditions and potential hazards, the dive teams carried their own light source while searching through the Swissair wreckage on the bottom. At best, underwater visibility would be about 10 m (30 ft), which is actually excellent for the waters around Nova Scotia, where a more usual limit is about 5 m (15 ft). Light is affected by the water's depth and falls off rapidly as one descends. The light level at 56 m (185 ft) is about one-third of what it would be at the surface. By the time a diver has descended to 91 m (300 ft), the surface light of a bright sunny day is displaced by an inky blackness.

Colour, too, is affected. Water acts as a filter, screening out the lower light frequencies first. At 4 m (13 ft) below the surface, the colour red has vanished, unless an artificial light is introduced. So a diver looking for a piece of equipment, such as the CVR or the FDR, which are orange, must now look for them as green, but only if they are in relatively shallow water. Green disappears at 9 m (30 ft). (Professional divers are trained to be suspicious of any smoky dark green or blue substance in the water around them because it could be blood.)

Plankton, a microscopic sea animal that is food for both smaller and larger denizens of the deep, also inhibited visibility on the bottom. The sheer volume of plankton in eastern Canadian salt waters can limit visibility to an average of 3 to 5 m (12 to 15 ft); therefore, a diver often was nearly on top of something before he would see it. In addition, shapes shift and waver in deeper water. Kelp swaying in the sub-currents, rock outcroppings, and mottled shapes created by sunlight and clouds overhead all can trick the eye, making an object seem to be there when it is not or vice versa. Another visual anomaly is that the bottom appears to rise up when it might be sloping down and away. The mind is easily duped when there is no usual reference to the horizontal and vertical.

Diving helmets worn during the underwater search not only protected the diver's head and breathing apparatus but also improved visibility. On Operation Persistence the divers used a fiberglass helmet called the

Superlite-17 that resembles a fighter pilot's helmet, but with a Plexiglas lens. A collar arrangement fits over the head and around the neck—dubbed the toilet seat by the divers because of its shape—attaches the helmet to the top of the diver's suit for a near-perfect seal against water. Inside the helmet, a mask covers the mouth and nose, freeing the divers from having a mouthpiece, which in turn allows to them talk to the topside crew. The head liner has earphones, which allow them to hear the support team.

Weighing 12 kg (27 lbs), the helmet has a robust brass handle bolted to the top on which a video camera is mounted, enabling those on the surface to observe exactly what the diver sees. To illuminate the area, a brilliant spotlight is mounted on the left side of the helmet opposite the video camera. Though this sounds cumbersome, it is quite compact.

Chief Adams was extremely pleased with the quality of the video pictures provided by this camera and called them "a godsend." They were capable of great depth of field; that is, they were in focus from very close to the lens out to a distance of nearly 3 m (10 ft) while providing a wide-angle view. Coincidentally, the cameras arrived only about a week before the disaster occurred.

In a sense, luck was with the divers on this particular site. As mentioned earlier, the visibility far exceeded the divers' expectations. Chief Petty Officer Glenn Adams attributed this clarity to the natural flushing action of St. Margarets Bay and the currents in the area. Whatever the reason, it was a badly needed break in an otherwise dangerous situation.

Safety was the watchword in Operation Persistence. Chief Petty Officer, Glenn Adams impressed on me during my interviews with him that the safety of divers and those ships' crews working with them was paramount in the recovery of remains and debris. He related conversations he had with relatives of crash victims, each of whom expressed concern for the safety of the divers and crews involved in the recovery operation. None of them wished to see further lives lost on account of their loved ones.

There was more than jagged metal that posed a threat to the divers' suits, their umbilical lines, and their own bodies. The water temperatures off Nova Scotia, even during the summer, are extremely cold. Although by September the surface waters are beginning to warm, this "warming" is only relative. There are places around this province that enjoy sea water temperatures of 20°C (70°F) or more due to location—shallow bays and coves with moderate flushing action or the influence of the St. Lawrence River for example—but the temperature drops sharply even a few hundred meters offshore. Below the surface, water temperatures also drop sharply, and at the depth of Flight 111's wreckage (57 m or 180 ft) the temperatures are near freezing.

To overcome the effects of cold waters, the divers wore two suits. The outer suit, called a dry suit, is constructed of thick neoprene rubber. This spongy rubber is a quarter of an inch thick on the outside with a tough nylon layer to help protect it against abrasions and cuts. The suits used by the navy divers had the added advantage of being heated. Rubber hoses with an inside diameter of about 1 cm were moulded into the insides of each suit. These carried hot water, pumped down from the surface, which circulated through tubes. They entered at the top of the diver's spine and spread down the spine to the legs and around the groin, and down the legs to the boots. The inner suit, one-eighth of an inch thick and also made was constructed similarly to the outer suit but without the hoses. When divers were fully suited, nearly a half-inch of neoprene was between their bodies and the water.

Because divers for Operation Persistence were working at such depths, they also required an oxygen/helium mixture to lessen the time they must decompress and to eliminate nitrogen narcosis. The latter arises when nitrogen that exists naturally in the blood reacts under pressures below 24 m (80 ft) or so, becoming toxic and in effect making the diver drunk. The use of helium eliminated the risk of nitrogen narcosis but introduced another. Helium is a naturally cold gas which, breathed into the lungs, tends to lower the diver's body temperature. It's this cooling effect on the larynx that distorts the voice and as we have seen can cause communication problems that have to be overcome electronically.

Time was of the essence once divers reached the wreck site. They had only 45 minutes on the bottom at about 55 m (180 ft), less the time back to the stage, to do their work. Once this time was up, they started their first ascent to 30 m (100 ft), which had to be accomplished in 2 minutes. There they waited for 1 minute of decompression time, then for every 3 m (10 ft) of rise they had to wait for another 3 minutes until they reached a depth of 18 m (60 ft), where they remained for 6 minutes. At 15 m (50 ft) they decompressed for 9 minutes; 12 m (40 ft) for 14 minutes; and 9 m (30 ft) for 30 minutes.

After this final wait, the divers were raised to the deck of the tender where their attendants quickly stripped off their gear and, as a precaution, hosed them down with a pressure washer to eliminate the possibility of contamination from human remains they encountered below. This strip down and cleansing was accomplished very quickly because the attendants had only 7 minutes from the time the divers left the 9-m (30-ft) level until they had to be in the recompression chamber. There they remained for 78 minutes on pure oxygen, with the remainder of time on air to a total of 172 minutes. In other words, the divers had to spend nearly three hours decompressing in order to accomplish about 37 minutes of work on the bottom. Unlike the recovery of the wreck of TWA Flight 800, most of which was in huge sections, the Swissair MD-11 was in millions of tiny pieces, all of which had to be gathered and brought back to the ocean's surface, if humanly possible.

On September 8, nearly six days after the crash of the Swissair plane, while searching the ocean bottom, two of the Canadian Navy's Clearance Divers located Flight 111's FDR. Since time was critical due to the pressures of weather, as well as the searchers' need to find

(D. Ledger)

Leading Seaman Paul Weber demonstrates the use of the Gas Mixing Console aboard the diving tender Granby. From this position, LS Weber controls the critical balances between oxygen, helium and CO_2 mixtures fed through the umbilical to the divers below.

answers for this tragedy—not only for the TSB and Swissair but for relatives of the victims—the divers on that day were using a different type of gear, what is sometimes called a closed-loop re-breather system. This re-breather system is an oxygen-helium mixture that allows some of the carbon dioxide exhaled by the diver to be fed through a scrubbing system that converts it into oxygen. The helium allows divers to breathe oxygen at depths greater than two atmospheres (20 m or 66 ft). This system allowed the divers greater freedom because they did not have to drag the umbilical all over the bottom and risk getting it slashed by the wreckage. Also less time was required to get back to the surface, which left more time on the bottom to locate the black boxes.

Alarmingly, while extricating the international orange FDR case from the debris, one of the divers slashed his dry suit. Immediately, near-freezing sea water began to seep in, not only causing extreme discomfort but threatening the diver's buoyancy. This sudden turn of events could have, in a matter of moments, become a life-threatening situation.

Still communicating topside, both divers were ordered to return to the surface. (It is foolhardy for one diver to remain in the water alone.) The diver with the damaged suit inflated his Buoyancy Compensator (BC)—a sort of life vest that counteracts the weighted-down diver, and fits around the neck, chest, and back. Nowadays these BCs are incorporated into the tank's back-pack, making up a single unit that can be put on as a whole. The navy divers working the Swissair site were on umbilical supply from the surface, so the tank was for emergency use only. Essentially the diver had become a human submarine, controlling descent and ascent.

The second diver, loath to leave the FDR on the bottom, snatched it up and, hugging it close to his body, inflated his own vest and tethered himself to the "damaged" diver to offset the weight of water in his suit. A swift ascent began. Suddenly, another life-threatening problem occurred. In hugging the black box to his body, the second diver had squeezed the re-breather bladder for the closed-looped system, expelling valuable mixed gas overboard. In doing so he had reduced his dive time to a factor far below what was needed to return to the surface in a routine fashion. Time was running out. One diver's suit was flooding, weighing him down and rapidly lowering his body temperature, and the other diver's atmosphere was rapidly depleting.

Topside, the *Granby* crew were standing by to recover the divers. In two minutes the divers reached the surface, twenty-eight minutes faster than normal. Once aboard the ship, the topside crew went to work. The two divers had to be stripped of their gear, hosed down, then rushed below deck to the hyperbaric (recompression) chamber, where they were locked in with a medical officer and repressurized to the depths from which they had just returned.

Fortunately, this emergency ended without serious injury to either diver. One of them suffered symptoms of decompression sickness, more popularly known as the bends; however, recompression alleviated the symptoms. The two divers were taken ashore and sent by ambulance to the Queen Elizabeth II Hospital in Halifax. They were released after a short stay but ordered to stay out of the water for two weeks as a precaution.

Now at least one of the two black boxes had been recovered. The CVR was still at large. There was a need to get to this as well before the power supply that fed its acoustical pinger failed, and there was nothing to say that this box was buried with the wreckage. It could have been well clear of it, half-buried in the gravel and sand bottom. Battling weather, time, and the hazardous depths and debris, the Clearance Divers continued recovering body parts while they searched for the elusive CVR.

(DND photo)

Two Canadian navy divers descend to the wreck site. Note the video cameras attached to the right side of their helmets.

Despite conditions on the ocean bottom, the dangerous debris, the hard work, and the distasteful task at hand, morale remained high among the divers, primarily due to their commitment to the relatives of the crash victims. The divers perceived that what they were doing would help the families in their grief over the long-term. The relatives wanted quick recovery and identification of their loved ones, and the divers were doing their best to accommodate them. It became their mission.

On Friday, September 11, three days after the FDR was brought to the surface, divers recovered the CVR. Though this would hopefully shed some light on the events that took place on the flight deck, the true contents would not be released to the public because Canadian law forbids it. Instead the TSB would provide only a summary of what had happened, if the tapes were useable.

During the excitement of the discovery of the CVR, HMCS *Preserver* steamed back to port. She had served as a floating morgue for nine days. Her captain and crew were heading ashore for a well-deserved break from what they described as a never-ending nightmare. Cmdr. Rick Town said the scenes aboard his ship over those nine days were more than one could imagine.

The *Preserver* was accompanied ashore by the Canadian Coast Guard vessel *Mary Hitchens*, which had stayed on station as well for those nine days. Her crew was also numbed by the experience. The trauma was telling. In one instance a crew member stubbornly refused to turn over a child's shoe until he was assured that it would be personally handed over to the child's relatives. A diary, a teddy bear, a woman's scarf, a Walkman, or a briefcase—items that were so familiar could stop crew members in their tracks.

All of this perhaps meant little to the divers, who had to continue the grisly operation of recovering body parts still twisted in the wreckage of the airplane, until Dr. Butt's pathology team was satisfied that they had identified all 229 passengers and crew aboard the flight. By September 14 the divers had made progress with the retrieval of remains: as much as two tons had been recovered.

(DND photo)

Leading Seaman Gulliford comes aboard with the CVR discovered on the bottom. The CVR is on the deck in front of the white coveralled crew member.

Eventually, the mission turned from the recovery of human remains to the recovery of the Boeing MD-11. The wheel trucks and flap actuators were lifted to the surface. The three engines and the relatively undamaged flap and slat tracks were located and brought to the surface. All these pieces were machined out of solid metal, so the likelihood of fragmenting during a 200-plus G impact was low. They would be extremely valuable to the topside investigators, as we shall see in later chapters.

Slowly and cautiously, because of the hazards involved in dealing with them, first the larger then smaller pieces of the airframe and hull were brought to the surface. Some of the pieces were as large as a kitchen table; however, most were not much larger than an adult's hand. Great care had to be taken to avoid further damage that could erase or modify trauma to the metal wiring or harnesses from the possible fire aboard or from the aircraft's entry into the water.

Weather and ocean conditions continually interrupted the divers' work. There were shutdowns, sometimes necessitating a retreat to shore. Then once more the vessels would head out, reposition and anchor, and begin the process. This was extremely time-consuming and tiring for crews and divers, but they kept at it.

After three weeks of diving—nearly a month after the crash of Flight 111—the TSB and the navy decided to cease diving operations. The weather was interfering more and more with their daily operations, and there were concerns about deep wave action endangering the divers' lives. They were also acting on advice and information received from the Bedford Institute of Oceanography (BIO), a large ocean sciences organization based on the Dartmouth side of Halifax Harbour.

Peter Smith heads up the Coastal Ocean Sciences section at BIO and was part of an environmental emergency team established after the crash of Flight 111. In 1986 Smith had done a study of winter ocean storms that begin off the Carolinas and the Virginia coast and how they intensify as they work their way north to the east coast of Canada. These storms traditionally begin to make their presence known about the middle of October—only six weeks after the Swissair crash and less than two weeks from the time the navy ceased diving operations. Smith discovered these storms, called bombs, can create deep currents that may extend downward as far as 50 m (165 ft) with speeds up to 1.8 kph (1 mph). That may not sound like much, but when you consider the average diver can sustain only about that same speed while swimming underwater, the current would be an exhausting and dangerous environment. In Smith's estimation, the loose wreckage still laying on the bottom—now contained in an area of about 30 by 70 m (100 by 230 ft)—could be scattered over thousands of metres, if not tens of kilometres, of sea bottom, and possibly lost forever to investigators. Smith's predictions and the La Niña-driven severe winter predictions for that coast combined to drive the TSB to consider any option available that would speed up the process without endangering lives.

The first option was the Remotely Operated Vehicles (ROVs). These little vehicles were tethered to the mother ship by an umbilical line, like their human counterparts. Electricity wasfed down the umbilical to power the lights, cameras, and all on-board equipment, including their electrically-powered engines. Signal impulses from above energized the vehicle's controls, the motors, and the grasping mechanisms. Video cameras transmitted images to a control area aboard the vessel. The ROVs were able to stay down for twenty-four hours at a time if necessary, picking up pieces of the MD-11, carrying them to waiting baskets, then dropping them in. The baskets were hoisted to the surface, quickly washed off and transported ashore to be taken to CFB Shearwater, where they would join the growing pile of wreckage that was once Swissair Flight 111. The Canadian Navy worked with ROVs for a couple of months, until they were down to smaller pieces of wreckage and debris scattered over an area of about two underwater acres.

Other than for maintenance or the lack of an operator, ROVs can continue for days, little affected by the harsh environment or the pressures of the deep. Because they were tethered to the surface, they were indirectly affected by the weather. If the surface vessel could not stay out in the weather, the ROV had to be brought aboard or risk possible loss due to the parting of the umbilical. At the cost of over $1 million apiece, the risk was not worth taking.

The navy completed their work with the ROVs and left the area around the end of October—at least until the spring. The TSB, still desperate to glean all they could from the site because they had not yet determined what caused the crash of Flight 111, commissioned the privately owned 120-ft Lunenburg scallop dragger *Anne S. Pierce* to dredge what she could of the wreckage for the rest of the fall, ceasing operations for the winter in late December. Fortunately, the potential havoc of the "bomb" storms didn't materialize, despite the winter storms that made their way along the eastern seaboard that winter.

The dragger returned and continued at the site into the spring of 1999, then the Canadian research vessel *Endeavour* came to the site with two ROVs in April. By then, 88 percent of the wreck of Flight 111 had been recovered. That left 12 percent of the wreck, by weight, on the bottom. To further complicate matters, during the course of earlier recovery efforts in February, another smaller debris field was discovered just east of the main wreck site in about 60 m (200 ft) of water. It was also in among rocks and ledges, making it difficult to access with the ROVs. Even if they could reach, it was thought that much of it was too heavy for the little unmanned subs to lift, and it was impossible to get at with scallop dragging techniques.

Once more the BIO came into the search with an invention of their own called a VideoGrab. Used to collect samples of sediment around ocean-going oil rigs and platforms from as deep as 500 m (1,650 ft), the apparatus was designed around a scooping mechanism and a video camera, and was capable of lifting about 500 L (2,300 Imp. gal) of sediment in one scoop. These ROVs proved to be an asset in the recovery of debris, some of which came from the nose section of the Boeing MD-11.

Debris recovery work continued through the summer of 1999, until all of the material that could be seen was brought up from the bottom. Still the Canadian TSB was not satisfied. A deep dredger, *Queen of the Netherlands*, equipped with a large sucking device that picks up material from the sea bed, was brought in to vacuum the bottom, collecting a half-metre or so of sediment, to ensure that everything had been brought to the surface. The barge, with the dredged cargo aboard, was towed to Sheet Harbour on the Eastern Shore of Nova Scotia, where it was pumped ashore through mesh screens into containment sections similar to those now built around large fuel storage tanks. Dikes were built up on the paved parking lot of a now-defunct marine engineering business. There, retired RCMP officers were hired to sift through everything, looking for more evidence of what caused Flight 111 to crash. A large shipment of diamonds was in the cargo hold of Flight 111, which is the suspected rea-

son that these retired RCMP personnel were hired.

At the time of writing, this was how the underwater search had ended, just over a year after Swissair Flight 111 dove into the Atlantic. It was the most exhaustive search ever for an airplane involved in a crash. So far, the search has cost over $85 million, and the investigation continues.

(TSB photo)

The TSB, in its final major sea operation to recover wreckage from Swissair Flight 111, used the trailing hopper dredge the "Queen of the Netherlands" to scour sections of St. Margarets Bay, during the last days spent searching the ocean floor in September 1999.

CHAPTER FOUR

Looking for Clues

Discovering the cause of the Swissair Flight 111 crash was going to be a Herculean task, and it fell to Canada, under the ICAO agreement, to provide the resources and bear the costs because the crash occurred in Canadian waters. As soon as the first human remains were pulled from the water and transported ashore in body bags, they were taken to CFB Shearwater for preliminary documentation and medical examination. CFB Shearwater is a quasi-military base about 45 km (37 mi) from the crash site—the base airport, incidentally, was closer to Flight 111's position than Halifax International and has a longer runway than the latter. Many of the military aircraft operating over the crash site the night of September 2 were staging out of Shearwater because it was so close, only ten minutes by air for a Sea King and less than that for a C-130 Hercules. Unfortunately, by the time Swissair declared an emergency, the possibility of getting to any airport was remote.

The federal government decided to use the base indefinitely for both the medical and TSB crash forensic teams. It was the obvious choice, not just for its close proximity to the crash site, but because it had everything the investigative teams would require. There were large, open, but protected, and heated working spaces; military security; a functioning military airport runway; the docks on Halifax Harbour; and military personnel on the base experienced in dealing with the mass movement of equipment, materials, and people. The base could provide food and sleeping accommodations on a moment's notice and there was a major city on its doorstep, offering many hotels and motels. With five universities, an oceanographic institute, and many companies specializing in marine sciences and technology all close by, the scene was set for an in-depth investigation into the crash.

If there is one single factor that impresses anyone who comes in close contact with the investigation of the crash of Swissair Flight 111, it is the apparent total destruction of the Boeing MD-11 aircraft as a result of its impact into the water off Peggys Cove. This was true of the searchers out on the water in the first hours after the crash, who had to plough through the floating debris looking for survivors, or remains. It was probably even more sobering to those searching after daylight from aircraft, for they would have had an overall view. And it was certainly daunting to the divers who had to retrieve the fragments from the depths.

The Players

The investigation of the crash of Swissair Flight 111 began almost immediately after the aircraft was lost from radar screens at Moncton Center. What began as a trickle of personnel quickly swelled to more than one hundred people from three countries. Most were from Canada but some were from the United States and Switzerland. As owner and operator of the airliner, Swissair sent maintenance workers and investigators from their National Aeronautics governing body. Since the MD-11 was built by an Americam company, the United States sent investigators from its National Transportation Safety Board (NTSB), as well as engineers, pilots, and aircraft fabricators from Boeing—the recent purchaser of McDonnell Douglas, the manufacturer of the MD-11. Under the ICAO Agreement— which in this situation requires that the country having jurisdiction of the crash perform the investigation, providing they have the expertise and resources to do so—Canada supplied the bulk of investigators and support personnel and bore the cost of the venture.

Another group entered into the investigation at the outset, remaining only long enough to satisfy themselves that the Swissair disaster was not the result of some outside agency. This group consisted of investigators from Interpol, the Federal Bureau of Investigation, and the RCMP and Canadian Transportation Safety Board (CTSB). The New York Port Authority and New Jersey were already looking into the event because the flight had originated there, and officials had begun interviews with the personnel at JFK Airport. The FBI, responsible for investigating any flight originating in the United States, initially downplayed any possible involvement by terrorists, though they did not rule it out. It seemed that Swissair was an unlikely target for a terrorist bomb. John Thompson, director of the Toronto-based MacKenzie Institute, which tracks violent groups and their activities around the world, remarked during an interview with Eva Hoare, a staff reporter with Halifax's *Chronicle Herald*, that "this crash doesn't bear the stamp of terrorists. A Swiss target would be unusual, it's not an American flag carrier. Terrorists don't make distinctions between military personnel and civilians, and airlines have been popular targets before." This held true with the CTSB as well, who were reluctant to put the face of terrorism on the crash, though they were initially unable to discount the possibility. All of the these agencies were constantly in touch with one another, exchanging whatever information they had.

Meanwhile, the search and rescue operation was gearing up off the mouth of St. Margarets Bay. Assets from both sea and air elements of the Canadian Armed Forces, the Canadian Coast Guard, and the Coast Guard Marine Auxiliary were among the first to be called and to arrive on site. Their involvement has been detailed in earlier chapters. These early rescuers retrieved remains and debris from the ocean, then transferred these to naval vessels on station, where they were transported ashore at Bayswater (because of its government wharf and its close proximity to the crash site) and held by the RCMP, or lifted by Sea Kings to CFB Shearwater. Later, the navy and Coast Guard opted to send their cargoes to Peggys Cove, which was closer to Halifax.

Pathology Investigation

Much has been made of the overwhelming task involved in discovering the identity of so many bodies and the trauma to those carrying out the task. Although this is true, local history would prove valuable in the approach to the daunting work ahead.

For instance, Halifax was the final location for 328 bodies recovered after the *Titanic* sank, and where many remain buried to this day. After that disaster, a Halifax coroner named John Henry Barnstead came up with a system, which is still in use, of identifying corpses. All personal belongings are grouped with the corpses, and each assigned a number. A detailed examination is made and notes kept with the body, including a photograph, descriptions, and sketches of tattoos and other personal markings. This information is then provided to police agencies and to relatives to help them identify their dead.

Nearly five years later, Barnstead's son made use of his father's system for a crisis closer to home. In December 1917, two wartime freighters, *Imo* and *Mont Blanc*, collided in the Narrows of Halifax Harbour. The *Mont Blanc*, loaded with Benzedrine and munitions, blew up and levelled North End Halifax, killing two thousand people. Marine disasters, mining disasters, and the carnage of two world wars have passed through Halifax military bases, docks, and morgues. So in September 1998, the children and grandchildren of those early disaster volunteers were put to the task once more.

A steady stream of ambulances and Sea Kings began arriving at Shearwater in the early hours of September 3. Leaves for base personnel were cancelled so an emergency receiving area could be assembled before the body parts began arriving. Personnel also had to set up temporary living accommodations and office space for the forensic people and kitchens to feed a steadily-expanding army of both military workers and civilians.

In a televised press conference on September 4 at CFB Shearwater, Dr. John Butt outlined the procedures that he had initiated and that his teams were following, in their attempt to identify remains from Flight 111. "On each team," explained Dr. Butt, "there is one doctor, one dentist. We have one radiographer, who manages on each team two radiographic technicians with an x-ray, one recorder, one experienced RCMP identification officer with a camera."

He appealed to relatives and families en route to Halifax to bring with them dental and medical records of the deceased, although he said the best way to identify these victims would be through DNA testing. Identifying bodies by "viewing" could be a flawed process, particularly when remains had been immersed in sea water for hours, possibly weeks.

Offers of help had been forthcoming from all over Canada and the United States, but at the time of the press conference, Dr. Butt admitted he'd been too busy to respond to most of these. Nevertheless, he said they were coping and that he was impressed with the morale and dedication of the team of fifty doctors, nurses, dentists, and technicians, most of whom had had little or no sleep in the previous forty-eight hours.

Although Dr. Butt had six teams set up to do the work, initially only two were working to identify remains, due to the absence of dental and medical records. In the meantime, the teams took x-rays and detailed examinations of recovered body parts. Three local hospitals sent x-ray equipment and staff to the makeshift morgue in Shearwater. Chris Power, the vice-president of nursing at Queen Elizabeth II Hospital, was concerned about a need for stress counselling for some of the x-ray technicians, who would not normally work with body parts. A steady stream of torsos, heads, and limbs began to trickle in—and the trickle soon turned into a torrent.

Within days, seven thousand police, volunteers, and military personnel were scouring hundreds of kilometres of convoluted and treacherous shoreline of the mainland and the little islands downwind of the crash site in search of more human remains and debris from Flight 111. Searchers had to thrash through dense brush and clamber over shoreline rocks slick with seaweed and algae. Sometimes a piece of wreckage would

(TSB photo)
Overhead view of the main wreckage hanger in Shearwater with wreckage laid out in groups.

be lifted to find human entrails attached to it or a limb hidden underneath. To further complicate things local sea life and shore creatures were taking advantage of this grisly harvest. Crash debris was being brought in, tagged and stored in boxes, and sorted out on table tops as the first steps of the TSB investigation got underway.

Two witnesses, a husband and wife living near New Harbour at the tip of the Aspotogan Peninsula, were shocked when they went to the beach a day after the crash. The tide had ebbed and searchers waded in thick piles of debris along the shore.

Debris was now washing up all around Mahone Bay and its little islands, making recovery difficult. A warning, couched in a request, was broadcast by the RCMP, asking the civilian population to bring anything they might find into local RCMP detachments. There were so many soldiers tramping around the area at Blandford that a sign was posted in the village declaring it CFB Blandford. In total, twelve hundred Canadian Army personnel and several hundred Ground SAR volunteers from all over Nova Scotia would be pressed into the search.

The Ground SAR, in some instances, gave up portions of their annual vacations or took time off work with loss of pay in order to carry out the enormous task at hand. One person I know of took his entire vacation allotment for that year, and some time donated by the company he worked for in order to spend a month scouring the shores of Mahone Bay and its islands.

For weeks this group of dedicated people searched the shores to the west of the crash site. They would be dropped off on small islands by boat or by helicopter to search and retrieve whatever they found, have it transported to shore-based locations, and return the next day to do it all again. Tides and fickle winds were not subject to human schedules and delivered their gruesome offerings to the shores in their own whimsical time.

By Thursday, September 15, indications were that the pathology teams in Shearwater had made considerable progress, evidenced by the following press release from the RCMP.

The Royal Canadian Mounted Police announced today that of the first 232 DNA samples collected from the crash site of Swissair Flight 111, DNA patterns representing more than 142 people (75 males and 67 females) have been established.

State-of-the-art technology has been used to analyze the samples and to establish genetic profiles of the individuals. Through comparison with the DNA obtained from family members and personal effects belonging to the victims, the task of identifying those killed on Flight 111 will be achieved. This undertaking, an unparalleled comparison of samples by DNA analysis in Canada, will take time to complete as additional samples are processed. To date, more than 192 reference samples from surviving family relatives which represent approximately 80 families have been provided to the RCMP.

Although unique to the individual, DNA acts as a genetic blue print [sic] which can link family members through a common pattern of inheritance passed down from mother and father to sons and daughters. It is this DNA link which will prove invaluable in the identification of those killed on Flight 111.

Within hours of the crash DNA specialists from the RCMP's forensic laboratory in Halifax, working in close cooperation with the emergency response pathology team, the Chief Medical Examiner for Nova Scotia, and other RCMP investigators, began the process of sample preparation for DNA analysis.

The major challenge of identifying the victims through DNA

analysis was given to the RCMP DNA Methods and Data Base Section in Ottawa and to the RCMP's forensic laboratories in Halifax, Regina and Vancouver. To date, the efforts of more than 25 RCMP DNA specialists working long hours have demonstrated that forensic DNA analysis is an effective tool for disaster identification, which will not only supplement conventional medical and physical procedures such as dental records, x-rays and fingerprints, but may provide, in some cases, the only source of identification for many victims.

The DNA investigation of Flight 111 is a major undertaking involving the cooperative efforts of numerous international and national experts. The expertise of the Center of Forensic Science in Toronto and the Armed Forces Institute of Pathology, Office of the U.S. Armed Forces Medical Examiner (Rockville, MD), as well as forensic DNA specialists involved in the crash of TWA 800 two years ago should be acknowledged for their support of this ongoing investigation.

In addition, the rapid response of the family members of the victims from 12 different countries and the coordinated efforts of RCMP investigators and Liaison Officers, as well as numerous other national and international agencies have been essential in the careful collection of reference DNA samples.

By December 15, 1998, Dr. Butt's team had identified 228 of the passengers on Swissair Flight 111—two passengers, identical twins, shared the same DNA. Identification of the 229 passengers was not meant to be construed as the ID of a body *per se* but of some part of a victim's anatomy that placed the individual at the scene of the crash. Labs across Canada had been involved in identifying fifteen hundred individual pieces of human remains in order to come up with a positive ID for each passenger. Most of the remains were returned to the families for burial, but there was still about 1,040 kg (2,300 lbs) of human remains, most of which was not identifiable and not matched to individuals.

It is not my intention to delve into the process of identifying the passengers and crew in the case of Swissair Flight 111. That has already been done in books such as Stephen Kimber's *Flight 111: The Tragedy of the Swissair Crash*. My concern here is what these remains contribute to the discovery of *why* this tragedy occurred in the first place.

The toxicology test findings have confirmed that there was no smoke in the passenger cabin of the aircraft. They did indicate that the aircraft's entry into the water was so devastating that the passengers were torn from their seats and jammed together to the point that their DNA was intermingled, making it even more difficult for the forensic pathology teams to identify individuals. The test findings also gave a clue as to the aircraft's speed at entry into the water. The passengers' intermingled DNA and the small wreckage area on the bottom confirmed that the aircraft went in nearly vertically. The significance of the plane's impact will be discussed in later chapters.

Transportation Safety Board Investigation

While the pathologists had their hands full identifying Flight 111 passengers, the TSB had its own problems with the vehicle of their destruction—the Boeing MD-11. Although there was no evidence of fire in the cabin, shortly after the discovery of the FDR and CVR the TSB decided that the flight deck and adjacent area behind it were the most probable source of a suspected fire that presumably caused the crash.

By this time the investigators had 640 boxes of debris recovered from the ocean bottom, skimmed from the ocean surface, and collected from shores. A large portion of this was housed in a specially and hastily erected structure dubbed "Hangar J," on the Tarmac about 300 m east of Hangar A at Canadian Forces Base, Shearwater.

I had the opportunity to tour Hangars A and J. Hangar J held boxes upon boxes stacked three tiers high in three long rows filled with countless bits of metal and debris. Hangar A was the primary sorting site for the wreckage of the MD-11, and a fenced-in area outside the building served as storage space for the three engines, the flap tracks, and slats, the wheel trucks and the few other large pieces of debris. Since winter was approaching, an annex was built in

(TSB photo)

Boxes and boxes—about 480 in all—of debris from Swissair 111 on the racks in Hangar "J" at CFB, Shearwater.

front of the hangar doors to act as a buffer so that the hangar wouldn't lose too much heat every time a door was opened. At the rear of Hangar A was an area reserved for Dr. John Butt's teams and for a bank of large refrigerator lockers on loan from the Canadian Navy.

The Flight Data Recorder

Much to the disappointment of the investigators, they were unable to recover any information from the FDR after the loss of radio transmissions from Flight 111 to Moncton Center. In fact, it appeared that every-

(TSB photo)
The Flight Data Recorder in a box filled with water to retard corrosion.

thing had ceased to operate aboard the aircraft about six minutes before it crashed. Everything, that is, except the engines and the flight controls. This was a blow, but it wasn't all bad news. Some data suggested that there was a progressive breakdown of equipment and instruments beginning a few minutes before Moncton Center lost contact with Flight 111. With at least this much to go on, investigators were determined to squeeze every bit of information they could from the two hundred-odd data sources that they did have.

Typical Flight Data Recorder Specifications

Time recorded:	25 hour continuous
Number of parameters:	5-300+
Impact tolerance:	3400Gs /6.5ms
Fire resistance:	1100 degC/30 min
Water pressure resistance submerged:	20,000 ft
Underwater locator beacon:	37.5 KHz
Battery:	6-year shelf life with 30-day operation

The FDR is a piece of sophisticated equipment, which taps into various flight instruments and sensors and records on a loop the status of dozens of data sources. Altitude, rate of climb/descent, time, speed, magnetic heading, attitude, various temperatures, G loadings, autopilot status, engine status are just some of the three hundred or so operational parameters monitored on most FDRs.

Swissair Flight 111's FDR was an L-3 Communications Corp. F1000 and could monitor 252 data input entries. It was mounted in the tail, far from the most logical impact point, was connected to the cockpit and other pick-up points by a wiring harness, and powered from a remote source. As with the CVR, if data-bearing and power cables are cut then equipment becomes redundant. Of course, the investigators have only the information recorded up to the time the wires were still intact.

The limited amount of time—twenty-five hours—that the data is readable before being recorded over has come into question, and the TSB has recommended that time be increased. (Both time extension recommendations made for the FDR and CVR will likely be implemented over the next five years with mandatory compliance by the year 2005.)

One might ask, if everything goes wrong in a matter of moments with instruments, controls, and engines, what is the point in having the FDR record what happened two or three hours earlier? The reason is that engine, electrical, and control problems quite often give indications early on of an irregularity that only later becomes obvious to the pilots. Little burps in the aircraft's performance might be telegraphing a potentially serious problem. That's fine if someone catches it, but if no one does and the aircraft crashes as a result, better still if the FDR captured the abnormality in its recording. This is particularly true if the FDR is disabled at the time of a crash, making it impossible to determine what happened.

Unlike their pilots, modern airliners do not get to lay-over and rest. They are in continuous use, stood down only to refuel or for maintenance. In the case of Flight 111, in the seventy-two hours previous to its departure from JFK, the aircraft had flown from Los Angeles to Zurich, then back to San Francisco, once more to Zurich, then to Singapore, then Jakarta, back to Singapore, on to Zurich, then over the Atlantic to JFK in New York. The cause of fire on Flight 111 en route to Geneva from JFK might have started many hours or days in advance of the event. It might also have been an intermittent failure, something that occurs briefly, then seems to cure itself but defies any effort to locate it and usually takes time to track down.

The missing six minutes on the FDR and the CVR might have been even more illuminating if data being sent to each had been received. Still, we are able to piece together at least a little of what might have happened in the last six minutes, as will be seen in chapter nine.

The Cockpit Voice Recorder

Although the FDR offered little insight into the cause of the crash, the TSB still had hopes of getting additional information from the CVR, recovered several days after the FDR. The CVR, a fairly straightforward piece of electronic equipment, is essentially a tape recording on Mylar metal-coated tape that recycles approximately every thirty minutes.

Cockpit Voice Recorder Specifications	
Time recorded:	30 minute continuous, 2 hours for solid state digital units.
Number of channels:	4
Impact tolerance:	3400 Gs /6.5ms
Fire resistance:	1100 degC /30 min
Water pressure resistance:	submerged 20,000 ft
Underwater locator beacon:	37.5 KHz
Battery:	6-year shelf life with 30-day operation

The CVR is very useful in that it not only will record the flight crews' conversations but also other noises or sounds in the cockpit. For example, it can hear the undercarriage being retracted, flaps being extended, air conditioning noises, various chimes, warbles, and enunciator warnings. Like the FDR if nothing happens to stop it from recording, it records over whatever is on the tape thirty minutes earlier.

About thirty years ago, the recording time was set at thirty minutes for CVRs. The crash of Swissair Flight 111 resulted in recommendations by the Canadian Aviation Safety Board that are being adopted by most aviation authorities throughout the world, who will subsequently regulate their air carriers. Extended to two hours, the CVR might more realistically determine whether there were events leading up to a disaster like the Swissair crash. The Safety Board was spurred on by the fact that Flight 111 was out of contact with Boston Center for thirteen minutes before it even entered Moncton's sector.

Though it has been reported that Boston Center did not pursue Flight 111's absence from contact in a controlled airspace, I for one do not believe it. In the closely monitored atmosphere of ATC, being out of touch is a serious breach of the regulations governing the passage of any aircraft through restricted airspace. If Flight 111 was ordered to change frequency, one of the pilots would have done so, then would have transmitted on that frequency to advise they were guarding that frequency, and received confirmation from ATC that they were being received. At the rate at which Flight 111

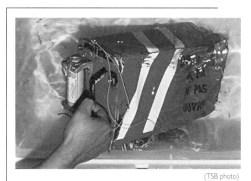

(TSB photo)

Cockpit Voice Recorder in water box.

was covering ground, being out of contact with Boston Center meant that the aircraft had gone about 130 miles through Boston's sector with only transponder and radar contact. Since there was only a thirty-minute loop on the CVR tape, the occurrence while Flight 111 was out of touch with Boston Center was not recorded.

This gap may have been nothing more than a frequency selector problem or a bad chip for the selected frequency. It is

(TSB photo)

Spaghetti-like pile of Mylar tape from the CVR and the Quick Access Recorders ready to be dried, cleaned and then played back by the TSB technicians.

even possible that the problem was with Boston Center's radio. Or it might have been a glitch in the wiring telegraphing a problem that was going to occur later. We might never know.

The CVR is usually mounted far back in the rear of the airplane to be as far as possible from the point of impact. Since the CVR is mounted so far back in the tail the microphone cable must run from the cockpit through the hull, usually between the outer skin and the interior, to the recorder nestled safely in the rear of the plane. If something cuts that cable, the CVR will not record. If the power feeding the box is cut, then the machine becomes redundant unless it carries its own power supply.

The equipment is normally surrounded by a waterproof case and is relatively secure in its location. The international orange case that it is housed in is not indestructible. In some crashes the box has split open and its contents have been exposed to high heat or water. The latter could have been the case with the Swissair CVR and FDR. Fortunately, despite its terrible impact into the ocean, Flight 111's CVR and FDR survived.

The media and the public were quickly disappointed by restrictions on the CVR findings. The TSB communiqué from Ottawa first gave a terse statement regarding the recovery of the CVR:

Cockpit Voice Recorder of Swissair Flight 111 Retrieved
(Halifax, Nova Scotia, 11 September 1998)
The Cockpit Voice Recorder (CVR) from Swissair Flight 111 has been recovered and is on its way to the Transportation Safety Board of Canada's (TSB) Engineering Branch Flight Recorder Laboratory in Ottawa, Ontario. The CVR has been placed in a container of fresh water and is being transported to Ottawa this evening.

The CVR was located and retrieved in about 54 m (180 ft) of water by divers operating from the *Granby* and was brought to the surface about 6:00 P.M. ADT. The CVR was recovered from a site near the location where the Flight Data Recorder was found on Sunday, September 6, 1998.

As soon as the Cockpit Voice Recorder arrives in Ottawa, work will begin to determine the condition of the Recorder and prepare it for playback.

Victor Gerden, Investigator-In-Charge, would like to thank the Canadian Forces Naval dive team for their perseverance and dedication in retrieving the CVR.

After detailing the recovery of the CVR, the following information was included:

Protection of CVR Information in Canada
...Canadian laws regarding the protection of CVR information conform with the ICAO standards for the conduct of aircraft accident in-

vestigation. However, under Canadian law (specifically the Canadian Transportation Accident Investigation and Safety Board Act), provisions require stricter protection for cockpit voice recordings and any transcripts from them than is practiced in some ICAO member states. In Canada, recorded CVR information is used strictly for the purpose of advancing transportation safety, and there are tight restrictions on access to it and on its use.

...[T]he Board may release to the public factual information specifically derived from the CVR to facilitate understanding of the accident flight in a timely manner. This may include confirmation of the presence or absence of specific events or activities at particular points in time; it may also include analysis of other cockpit ambient noises such as engine or mechanical sounds. The investigators will not be releasing any transcript of the recorded information in any form to the public, but information from these recordings will be used by a multi-disciplinary team of investigators to help identify safety problems. Any safety deficiencies requiring urgent attention will be dealt with promptly.

In summary, Canadian laws respecting the protection afforded to CVR information give primacy to using only that information necessary to advancing aviation safety, while protecting the privacy of the crews whose voices may be heard on the tapes.

This was a blow to the media, who were depending on this information to round out their stories and perhaps discover new ones to present on the six o'clock news. It did not stop the American press. The *Wall Street Journal* later released a story providing leaked details of an alleged discussion—presented by the paper as more of an argument—between the pilot and co-pilot about dropping procedures and heading straight for Halifax International.

When Victor Gerden, of the TSB, held a press conference, he downplayed this information and reiterated the law concerning the release of recorded cockpit conversations. He also disputed allegations that the flight crew was arguing. Gerden allowed there might have been discussion between the two pilots but would not entertain the possibility that the co-pilot would openly argue with his captain.

Regardless, by September 15 the TSB had determined that the CVR was going to be of no immediate help in determining what happened during the last six minutes of the flight.

The Nose Section Mock-up

The first real evidence of heat damage or fire began to show up in November. In a press release dated November 20, 1998, the TSB stated:

> The recovery operation continues to raise aircraft material that shows varying amounts of heat distress. The heat-damaged material includes a few small pieces of melted aluminum, from the ceiling area just aft of the cockpit door. Other signs of heat damage include some electrical wires with melted copper, arcing damage, and charred or missing wire insulation. The sheepskin fabric on the observer seat, located in the cockpit behind the pilots' seats, has a few drops of imbedded melted plastic. A few small pieces of metalized Mylar show discoloration from exposure to heat. The heat-damaged material found to date is located in the forward upper area just forward and aft of the cockpit bulkhead. The damage is consistent with a localized high heat source or a localized fire in this section of the aircraft. To date, there are no signs of fire in any other section of the aircraft.

The cause of the fire, or high temperature heat-stress, was still eluding investigators. In the Engineering Lab in Ottawa the forensic investigators were exposing the same types and gauges of wiring used in the MD-11 to varying degrees of heat, then quenching them in salt water in order to determine what heat was present to cause the damage and discolouration seen on wires recovered from the wreckage. By using spectral analysis and electron microscopes, they could determine, within a few degrees to what temperatures wires had been exposed.

Investigators performed the same type of experiments with bits of metal of the same type, thickness, and age from elsewhere on Flight 111's hull, then compared them with metal from the cockpit that showed evidence of heat distress. By careful treatment of the metals with heat and saltwater quenching, they were able to determine the heat produced in those areas of the cockpit that had the greatest damage. Once they could definitively determine this, they could narrow the investigation to that area and to the possible cause of the fire.

In order to probe the cause and source of heat, investigators were first going to have to find all material, or at least most of it, and then identify where it came from on the cockpit's hull. The idea was to piece these suspect metals together, along with associated suspect wiring in a specific area. Knowing what equipment was in what area could help determine the cause of the fire. The investigators were going to require something three-dimensional something they could work on from the inside as well as the outside. They decided to do what has been done for forty years in the aircraft investigation field: they would build a framework of the MD-11 nose section and lash the pieces to that. The framework would be built to the same dimensions and shape as the original nose of the aircraft. It would be constructed of steel tubing and steel mesh. This would not only include the outer aluminum skin of the aircraft but any plastic interior soundproofing, cladding, instrumentation, and, most importantly, any wiring discovered in the debris.

(TSB photo)

A framework duplicating the nose section of the MD-11 was constructed and transported to Hangar A in Shearwater. Various pieces of wreckage from Flight 111's nose section were attached to it in an attempt to discover the area where the fire began and spread.

Nova Scotia's Department of Highways was given the task of constructing the mock-up. The structure was welded together at one of their facilities at Miller's Lake near Halifax International Airport. Upon completion, the cage-like model was transported on a flatbed to Hangar A at CFB Shearwater. There it was mounted on a large plywood staging and fastened into place, a steel skeleton awaiting its tattered and twisted cladding.

Usually each piece of metal bears an identification code stamped in ink or written in indelible pen or tagged with a riveted metal ID number during manufacture to locate it on the aircraft's airframe when it is built. With the plans supplied by the manufacturer—in this case McDonnell Douglas—TSB investigators aided by RCMP personnel began to fit what pieces they had found to the fabricated jig. The work ahead would be challenging.

From the MD-11 plans, they were able to determine that there were approximately 5,000 pieces of material making up the nose of the aircraft. They had nearly half a million pieces that had been recovered to go through to find those five thousand—and the other half of the aircraft was still on the bottom of the Atlantic. To make matters more difficult the suspected fire location in the aircraft's nose was in the one area that received the most devastating impact during the crash. It was known, by this time, that Flight 111 had literally demolished itself when it went into the water vertically and at considerable speed. The nose was the first to hit and, in addition to the MD-11's speed, had the weight of the remainder of the aircraft—nearly 360 tons—behind it. It was suspected that the MD-11, upon entry into the water, hit a ledge about 15 m down before continuing its descent to depths of about 55 m.

Silent Witnesses

Over the last fifty years or so, aircraft accident investigators have come to rely on "silent witnesses" (my term) to help them solve cases in which the reason for an accident is not readily apparent. These silent witnesses—what the investigators refer to as witness marks such as telltale dents, scratches, or abrasions on any piece of the aircraft that might have been in use during the crash—can be mechanical in nature, and are usually the product of some stress, force, or trauma to machinery, instrumentation, and the structure of the aircraft, both during the flight and just before the aircraft crashes, in the exact moment of impact and those several seconds after the impact, when the aircraft is still in motion.

Aircraft investigators all over the world have contributed to this forensic science in many ways since the British began seriously investigating airliner crashes after the in-flight destruction of several of their DeHavilland Comets—the first true jet airliner—during the late 1950s. What happened to these aircraft would have remained a mystery had British investigators not begun to look at these crashes from a scientific and engineering point of view. Their positive results spurred other countries to pursue this avenue of investigation to further increase knowledge in this field.

In the case of Flight 111, the flap actuator pistons—the rams extended hydraulically to extend or retract the flaps at the trailing ends of the wings— were partially extended when the aircraft plunged into the water. The stress on the flaps during entry forced the lip on the outer casing of the actuator against the chrome-plated piston, leaving a slight dent in the piston. The position of this mark indicated that the flaps had been extended fifteen degrees when the airplane crashed. Flaps provide high lift capability at slower speeds and are usually used during takeoff and landings. They are also used when the aircraft has to stay within an area. In the case of Flight 111, the pilots were using the flaps for better stability while flying at an average speed of 318 knots or about 600 kph (375 mph), much slower during the banking turns around St. Margarets Bay than the FDR indicates is the usual flying speed of about 880 kph (550 mph).

The recovered slat tracks and actuators indicated that the leading edge slats were not extended as indicated. Had they been extended, which they usually are when main flaps are also extended, that would have provided the pilots with further lifting capability at their slower speeds. It is curious that they were not. It is possible that they had been extended but refracted on their own when electrical power failed. This could have been the result of loss of electrical power, possibly a default situation resulting in a loss of signal to whatever processor failed when the power stopped. The slats would then have retracted on their own or were never deployed at all. But the pilots presumably had control over them and could have switched off the deploying mechanism.

I mention the leading edge slats because there have been slat problems on the MD-11. They were the cause of another MD-11 incident a couple of years earlier, so were an immediate target for speculation. However, it is unlikely they had anything to do with the cause of Flight 111's crash. This is not to say that leading edge slats were not in some way responsible for difficulties in controlling the aircraft during the last six minutes. Rather, they might have been an effect rather than a cause. In any event, slats would have been investigated so as to eliminate them as a probable cause, or a contributing cause.

If there was total power failure aboard the aircraft, pumps supplying power to the hydraulic actuators, the ailerons, the rudder, the elevators, the spoilers, and even the landing gear would have been cut as well, leaving the pilots with little control over their aircraft. Nowadays, however, each airliner is equipped with a little pump driven by a 1-m (4-ft) long propeller; during a loss of hydraulic pressure, a sensor activates a mechanism that causes the pump to drop down out of the belly of the aircraft. The pump is driven by the propeller spinning in the slipstream, supplying enough hydraulic pressure to give pilots control over the primary flight controls. Though the MD-11 had an electrical link from the control column to the flight controls, there was also a physical link between the control column and the control surfaces via hydraulic activation. Had this not been the case the pilots would have had no control of the aircraft's control surfaces, such as the ailerons, rudder, or elevators, hence they would not have been able to control the airplane.

(TSB photo)

Mostly intact, though heavily damaged, Engine Number One rests on the floor of Hanger J in Shearwater. Note the section on the left side of the photo which shows the hub devoid of the impeller blades that were once part of the rotor.

Since there is speculation that Flight 111 was without any electrical power to its instrument panel for the last six minutes of its flight, the systems dependent on that panel could have failed as well, even the fuel pumps. There were seventeen of them on the MD-11, used to supply the engines and to transfer or boost fuel from one area to another, helping to maintain the airplane's critical center of gravity (balance). Engines no. 1 and 3 were gravity fed, as mentioned previously, and were below the fuel source of the main wing tanks. Number two engine, high up on the tail, was dependent on electrically-driven pumps to supply it with fuel.

During a 200 G entry into the water witness marks left on the shafts and other moving parts of the pump might determine which ones were working at the time, and from which voltage bus. These pumps are still being analyzed. Knowing which voltage busses were still in operation could determine what instruments were still functioning in the cockpit. "When something stops quickly or rubs against something when it stops quickly or is crushed," explains Jim Harris, the Public Relations Officer with the TSB, "it usually leaves what is called a witness mark, and if the pump was turning, it would leave a different type of witness mark from a pump that wasn't turning. If we can determine which pumps were operating and which ones weren't, that may tell us which electrical systems were or were not operating at the time."

Non-volatile memory chips—chips that don't rely on electrical energy to maintain their memory—from the Full Authority Digital Engine Controller (FADEC) have been recovered from the three Pratt & Whitney PW4462 engines on the Swissair MD-11. There is information on these chips, but unfortunately there is no timeline reference, so the investigators have no way of knowing what time period—before or during the crash—information was recorded.

Instruments still being used as G-forces may also be valuable to the investigators. The Air Speed Indicator (ASI) or Mach Meter, for instance, would have been recording airspeed up to impact. At the point of impact, the needle would have slapped into the face of the dial with sufficient force to leave a witness mark on the dial, indicating the speed at impact. The Attitude Indicator (AI) would likely have frozen in the attitude the aircraft was in when it hit the water, if it did not tumble before impact.

The investigators and lab technicians in Ottawa have other tricks up their sleeves to find clues to the cause of the crash. For example, the Engineering Lab's Electrical Analysis Section had pioneered the science of determining stresses imposed on an aircraft by studying the effect of high Gs on heated lamp filaments. These lamps are used for general lighting and are found in all sorts of equipment, such as indicators and enunciators. The white-hot and malleable filaments twist, stretch, and break in predictable fashion when encountering high stress such as a crash. The Engineering Lab had catalogued hundreds of these little bulbs and their behaviour under varied conditions. Knowing these behaviours could help determine what forces were at work during impact, or whether a particular warning light was on when the aircraft impacted. And knowing which warning light was on could point to a trouble spot that led to the crash. In fact, there has been recent speculation that the map reading light, overhead in the cockpit, might have been the initial source of the electrical malfunction.

Non-mechanical articles may also reveal important information about the crash. For instance, the aircraft maintenance documents, forwarded from Swissair, would be carefully gone over by the Document Analysis Section of the RCMP outside Ottawa. They would begin examination with the naked eye, then use light-enhancing equipment called a Video Spectra-Comparator. This uses colored lighting, including ultra-violet and infra-red, which causes various inks to fluoresce, thereby determining if anything was amiss during maintenance procedures. The experts could detect changes in the ink used to overwrite a previous entry in the log, for instance, or detect an erasure. Analysis of the paper fibers could determine if they had been heavily imprinted upon in an attempt to disguise or negate an earlier entry.

To illustrate, a chartered Canadian DC-9 carrying passengers to Nigeria took off from Jiddah, Saudi Arabia, on July 11, 1991. Ground personnel noted that there was smoke pouring out of the belly of the aircraft. They reported the smoke to flight crew, who turned the aircraft back to land. Twelve minutes after the flight took off, it crashed in the desert a short distance from the runway, killing all 264 people on board. It was later determined by a Canadian forensic investigative crew, that on takeoff a tire had failed, fragmented, and then jammed the wheel hub bearings, causing the hub to scrape along the runway and overheat. The remainder of the rubber tire caught fire. The flight crew—completely unaware of the situation—retracted the gear into the inboard wheel wells, below the passenger cabin and behind a fuel tank. A fire ensued that burned a large hole into the cabin, through which some passengers fell while the aircraft was still in flight. The subsequent investigation into the maintenance documents revealed the tire pressure on that (and one other) tire was 11 kg (25 lbs) below standard but that the information in the maintenance log had been overwritten to make them appear up to standard.

In the case of Flight 111, all documents, including those recovered from the wreck, would have been scrutinized by the investigators—initially the RCMP—first of all to determine if the passengers had noticed anything unusual during the early part of the flight and noted it in a diary or notebook. Another reason would be to look for written evidence of a personal or political mission, such as a suicide or hate crime. Documents recovered from the water were restored by vacuum freeze-drying—a process that vapourizes water, allowing the moisture to evaporate quickly from the paper and restores near pulp to the document's original condition.

Contrary to the opinion of some that the cockpit was vacant when Flight 111 crashed, investigators were able to determine—by the stress forces imposed by seat belts on the belt connections to the seat itself—that both pilots were in their seats at impact Abrasions to material worn by the pilots showed damage consistent with what would be caused by seat belts worn during a high G impact, and twisted metal parts from the seat also showed this type of stress. In addition to this, spray patterns of both plastic and metal on one seat and the surrounding area indicate that these seats were occupied during contact. The jump seat, situated behind the centre console, showed a spattering of molten material, while the pilots' seat material showed no such spattering.

As previously mentioned, toxicology samples taken from the remains of the pilots and passengers were used to eliminate the possibility that there was a fire in the passenger compartment, and to see if pilots were subjected to some degree of smoke inhalation. Since both men were wearing oxygen masks, there was little chance of them being asphyxiated by cockpit fumes generated by burning plastics. Even the fire extinguishers were examined, five of which were discharged, but there was no conclusive proof that they were used to fight a fire.

Although there are no firm conclusions of what actually happened during the last fateful six minutes, data collected from the CVR and FDR, the radar, and memory-chip information if it's found, along with evidence gleaned from the lights, instruments, and documents, will all eventually reveal their secrets.

Theories About the Crash

There were some large pieces of the MD-11 recovered intact, including the tires, which still had air in them. The landing gear trucks and the engines, though badly damaged, were scattered among wreckage on the ocean bottom. There were other machined and aluminum parts—such as flap extension rails and landing gear hard points—that survived relatively intact. The piston-like flap actuators were in one piece and are a valuable find because they could tell a story on their own. But the rest of this Swissair MD-11 seems to have been blasted to bits.

When investigators and rescue workers became familiar with the crash site, there was one paramount question on their minds: What could have caused such devastation? Even before the investigation had begun, there was speculation that an explosion might have caused the loud "thunderclap" reported by many witnesses in the area. And the cockpit communication with Halifax Terminal Control at Moncton Centre had ended abruptly. This had the media—and probably the TSB and the RCMP—wondering about the possibility of a terrorist bomb. Indeed, the recent history of terrorist-plotted air disasters would have triggered concerns by such agencies as the FBI and RCMP as a matter of procedure.

The 1988 crash of a Pan Am Boeing 747 over Lockerbie, Scotland, caused by a terrorist bomb, and the 1996 TWA Flight 800 crash in the Atlantic just miles from New York City—killing all 259 people on board— were still fresh in everyone's mind. The TWA Flight 800 investigation had been closed only recently, and, although a bomb was first suspected, it was finally concluded that an electrically-caused explosion in a forward fuel tank was the probable cause of the crash. The source of the electric spark that is supposed to have ignited fumes in one of the plane's giant gas bays has not been found.

And there was still speculation about the December 12, 1985 crash in Gander, Newfoundland, where a chartered Arrow Air DC-8 went down, killing 256 people. Members of the American 101 Airborne Division were returning for Christmas from duty in the Middle East; the crash has never been resolved to the satisfaction of the relatives of those killed. And it remains a blight on the record of the Canadian Aviation Safety Board, the forerunner of the Canadian Transportation Safety Board.

Having said all that, the facts in the 1998 Swissair crash do not support the theory of a powerful explosion in the air. Despite losing radio contact with Flight 111, radar at Halifax and CFB Greenwood were still painting the MD-11 on their screen. They followed the aircraft, still in flight, for nearly six minutes until its altitude dropped below 2,000 ft and the radar on top of Aylesford Mountain north of CFB Greenwood lost it. Not long after, the radar at Halifax lost the target below low hills on the Halifax Peninsula, southwest of the radar's location at 610 ft. In fact, Halifax had the MD-11 on screen until about twenty seconds before impact. Whether the plane was still under control during this time and after loss of radar contact is open to conjecture, but because of the time it took for the plane to come down it appears that it was intact. The bomb theory was discounted once it became known that the aircraft contacted the water completely intact.

Toward the end of its flight, the aircraft was flying erratically down the east coast of St. Margarets Bay, coming close enough to the land to be almost over Indian Harbour. The aircraft then veered to its right and began a roughly flattened circle, which brought it over the south tip of the Aspotogan Peninsula, then briefly back out to sea before it hit the water about 10 km to the east of that land mass.

So what was the reason that this 250-ton aircraft was found within a fairly small area of the ocean floor in hundreds of thousands of small pieces? It is not likely to have been a gas explosion upon contact with the water because of the speed of entry and the dowsing effect of water on a gasoline explosion. It is known that the emergency arose in the cockpit and that, although fire is suspected there, it was well away from the fuel tanks, housed in the main and tail wings, and in the lower fuselage between the main wings.

I have given this a great deal of thought and, based on my knowledge of pressurization and what can happen when gas compresses, I ran my explosion theory by Larry Vance, the Deputy Director at TSB under Victor Gerden. "Could it," I asked, "have been hydrodynamic pressure that blew Flight 111 to pieces?" I wondered if the aircraft's speed upon impact, the incompressibility of the water outside and the compressibility of air inside had combined to turn the interior

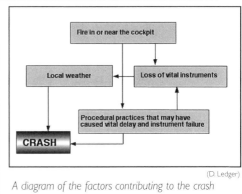

(D. Ledger)

A diagram of the factors contributing to the crash of Swissair Flight 111.

of the fuselage into a bomb. Vance agreed; that was what the Safety Board were assuming had caused the explosion. Compression in the fuselage, caused by the downward speed, had blown the aircraft into tiny pieces as it was entering the water. The water itself—as hard as concrete to an object hitting the surface at such great speed—had entered and demolished the forward section of the MD-11.

As I probed into the crash of Swissair Flight 111, it became clear that there were four components contributing to, and resulting in, this tragedy: first, cockpit smoke and fire; second, loss of electrical power; third, pilots' procedural practices; and fourth, the local weather. The sequence of these four components as chapters in this book is somewhat arbitrary, and serves only to simplify a discussion of what probably occurred before this crash. One should keep in mind that these components are, in fact, complex and interrelated. Each of these factors is discussed in detail in the next four chapters. In this chapter, I've elaborated on the Transportation Safety Board's's findings concerning events that unfolded on the flight deck during the fifteen minutes preceding loss of communication between Flight 111 and Air Traffic Control. What follows is my own speculation about what actually happened and what we haven't been told about the crash of Flight 111.

Smoke in the Cockpit!

To date, the overwhelming facts support the theory that smoke in the cockpit started the chain of events leading to the crash of Flight 111. Since Captain Zimmermann called in a Pan Pan Pan to Moncton Center and indicated that there was the smell, then the sight of smoke, we must proceed on the assumption, at least for now, that there was a fire close by. Its cause, however, has not been confirmed since vital aircraft material from around the critical area has not been identified.

There were indications early on in the investigation by the TSB that this may have been a fire in the wiring harness for the newly installed inflight entertainment system comprised of the movie delivery system and the audio entertainment feeds to the seats in the passenger compartment. The theory was strong enough for TSB to issue a bulletin advising inspections of the entertainment system aboard any aircraft using an Interactive Technologies System. Months later the Federal Aviation Administration (FAA) issued an order to have all such entertainment systems disabled or removed in all American carriers. Swissair has gone so far as to begin legal proceedings against the American company, Interactive Technologies Inc., which installed the entertainment systems. Whether the wiring job was at fault will be hard to prove without the necessary wires as evidence. So far, the CTSB has only said the area around this system is suspect but has not specified it as the cause.

There is a saying in the computer sector of the technology business: "Garbage in, garbage out." This might apply here: "garbage in" would be faulty electrical materials, "garbage out," the resulting electrical fire. It could well be that the entertainment system eventually caused a fire just because it was drawing current from the MD-11's voltage buses, but if one of those buses were faulty in the first place, the company can hardly be blamed for the fire that resulted. When installing the new equipment, they would assume that the buses were sound. It would not have been their responsibility to check the voltage buses and they would have no way of knowing otherwise and would have complied with the regulations concerning installation of the system. It is now known that Kapton wiring— the wiring used in the MD-11—is an excellent wire as long as it doesn't chafe, have tight bends, or vibrate too much, certainly a short-coming for aircraft installation. Drawing current through aging Kapton wiring to supply the latest addition to the aircraft entertainment system is akin to climbing a ladder with some of the higher rungs sawn partially through. And if, during the course of installing this equipment, the technicians somehow damaged existing wiring harnesses or routed wiring in such a way that it might cause chaffing, that would be akin to installing a time bomb.

A portion of Interactive Technologies' entertainment system aboard an MD-11 aircraft, similar to Swissair Flight 111.

There are numerous clues to support the theory that there was a fire in or near the cockpit, not the least of which are the pilots' reports of smoke and reference to smoke on the CVR. In addition is the discovery, during the investigation that some of the recovered cockpit material indicates were exposed to very high heat. In particular is a section of wiring harness from the cockpit, which is extremely brittle due to its exposure to high temperatures. Other indications of extreme heat include molten plastic from the overhead panel, which was deposited on the jump seat, which is behind the centre console separating the two pilots, in the cockpit. In addition there are pieces of metal from around the cockpit that show extremes in temperature exposure.

We also know that, following standard procedure, the pilots had donned their oxygen masks soon after they smelled smoke in the cockpit. If the smoke on the flight deck was extremely thick, which could easily have been the case with Flight 111, this in itself might have been enough to impair the pilots' ability to see their flight instruments, never mind being able to see ground details, such as lights that—when their instrumentation was lost—would allow them to keep the plane level.

In any event, within minutes the situation was serious enough for the pilots to declare an emergency. Pilots, it should be noted, have an enormous resistance to declaring emergencies when in flight because of the lengthy investigations and paperwork that follows, and the cost to the airlines of any protracted delays. Almost certainly any aircraft declaring an emergency will be grounded for days, perhaps weeks, resulting in a loss of revenue to the company on top of the cost incurred for an inspection. If an emergency is declared because of the presence of smoke in the cockpit, and it turns out to be just some vapour from an air conditioner (not an uncommon occurrence) the pilot's competence will be called into question.

Kapton wiring has been identified by many as the real culprit in this accident. Aromatic Polyamide Tape Insulation, the covering surrounding the wire core, manufactured under the name Kapton by DuPont, has been in some of the carrier fleets since the early seventies. Even then it had it's dissenters. Outspoken opponents of the material repeatedly warned the FAA about using this type of wiring in aircraft. During the eighties the United States Navy removed this wire from their F-14 Tomcats and some of their Carriers due to its volatile nature. The Lockheed-P3 Orion was also affected; and the Canadian Air Force removed the offending wire from the same aircraft by another name—the Aurora—their long-range patrol aircraft used for submarine detection, maritime patrols, and SAR in a program that ended a few years ago. It was known among some airlines that the wire cable could chafe, causing arcing in the movable sections of the passenger seats.

Kapton, as already mentioned, is a good wire if it is run properly. It conducts well, and is one-third lighter than a comparable wire, so it has an excellent weight for current carrying capability—that is, if it doesn't chafe or ring-split (crack open around its circumference) during its operational lifetime in an airplane. But the fact is that the most common cause of maintenance problems in any aircraft is vibration. Vibration causes all sorts of fatigue in the airplane's metal skin, its engines, its electronic equipment—and in its wiring.

So, ironically, we have a material that is prone to cracking when fatigued due to vibrations, and that becomes volatile if cracked in one of the most vibration-prone machines of our age. Airplanes continuously flex, stretch, and twist in flight; during pressurization the hull stretches and flexes. The wings exert tremendous torque, compression, and sheer tension on the fuselage, which, of course, is built to take it, but everything in the aircraft is affected by all of these micro-movements, sometimes thousands of times per second. We feel them as vibrations. Any wiring that is resting against, strung across, or wrapped around these vibrating parts and sections can be chaffed, stretched, or twisted right along with them. A cable such as Kapton is going to suffer and is bound to fail, sooner or later, as a result.

This is not to say that the wiring in an aircraft, particularly an airliner, is run in a haphazard fashion. It isn't. Precautions have always been taken to counter the effects of vibration, stretching, and twisting. When an airliner is being built, its wiring is combined into harnesses, and the cable is carefully laid out round and across the hull to best facilitate the function powered by electricity.

A bundle may be made up of twenty or thirty wires; some of them are thick enough to carry heavy currents, while others might be simply signal carrying cables with barely discernible currents. These bundles are carefully strapped together by bundle wraps, run along the hull to a particular point, then fixed firmly to the hull or a stringer or bulkhead by some type of insulated standoff or clamp, which in turn is usually insulated. Bundles are insulated, given slack, and looped or coiled to combat rubbing, flexing, or twisting.

photo courtesy of http://members.aol.com/papcecst/

The burning of MIL-W-81381/11 wires which were ignited when circuit breakers were reset.

Careful attention is given to the lengths of each cable and bundle and their contact points, their location against the side, top, or bottom of the airplane, and whatever they pass through or around.

All of these harnesses—and there are dozens of them, some long, some short—are then buried out of sight behind sound and heat insulation and the cosmetic shell on the aircraft's interior. One can appreciate why the airlines would be reluctant to replace all of this wiring in their carriers if there is only a slight chance that a fraying or a break might occur in some wire's insulation.

However, this reluctance has to be tempered by what is now known, and some argue has always been known, about Kapton wiring. It is now suspected by knowledgeable people in the industry that many crashes in the past have been caused by faulty wiring rather than by the failure of equipment. The crash of Swissair Flight 111 has shone a very bright light on aircraft wiring and its likely contribution to dozens of airplane crashes during the history of general aviation. If this connection proves true, it will no doubt have a dramatic effect on some of the world's major air carriers. Most modern passenger-carrying aircraft built over the last twenty to twenty-five years boast about 250 km (150 mi) of wiring throughout their structures. Many of these aircraft are wired with Kapton wire.

I viewed a videotape of a test carried out by the United States Navy on Kapton cable in some of their military aircraft. A wire bundle was linked to a power source, fed through a series of circuit breakers, and attached to a load representing the equipment they would feed when in place in an aircraft. In this case, a .50-calibre bullet was fired through the bundle of wires, simulating combat conditions. When the bullet was fired through the wiring harness, there was a brief flash of light as the wires shorted out. As a result, many of the affected circuit breakers did their job and popped out, rendering those circuits useless and depriving the wires of voltage. But when the individual wires shorted out, they sizzled and sputtered, spraying little molten balls of copper and steel in close proximity to the wire bundle. Eventually the reaction stopped. This was uncharacteristic of normal wiring.

The second part of the procedure was to reset the circuit breakers, as is standard procedure, to see if there were any chance of revitalizing the piece of affected equipment and get its information back on-line. An even more startling thing happened. Rather than powering up the simulated equipment load, the affected wiring began to flash-over—in other words, to conduct current on the insulation of the wire—despite the fact that the actual wires in the cables were severed and no longer capable of carrying current. To make matters worse, once the cable flashed, it continued to conduct current and support combustion at the same time. In fact it acted like a slow match, a type of fuse used to detonate explosives. As long as the circuit breaker was closed, the wire continued to burn with an intense flame and at a temperature later concluded to be in the range of 5,000°C.

Under certain conditions Kapton hydrolyzes, which means it absorbs water, causing it to expand, which in turn causes cracking and peeling.

Once this happens and the wire comes in contact with other metals—such as the metal hull, another wire bare from chaffing, or the metalized layer of the aircraft's Mylar soundproofing and heat insulation—there is an instant shorting out. If there is a heavy current flowing through the hydrolyzed wire, the scene is ripe for disaster. Once the reaction starts, the insulation begins to blacken and creep, or to shrink back along its metal core. It will burst suddenly into flame, which is sustained until the circuit breaker pops, cutting current to the affected wire.

One only need look at the wire harnesses of older commercial aircraft to see some of the inherent problems that contribute to electrical failure. Dust accumulates on the cables, held there by static attraction and years of adhesion by various agents used to clean, lubricate, or combat corrosion on the outer hull. By osmosis, agents used to clean the passenger cabins, particularly those that are suspended in the air, will to some degree make their way through the cosmetic inner wall to the exterior hull and the wiring harnesses. This along with dust, fabric microparticles, and human skin particles accumulate on the wiring. A hairline crack anywhere along a wire carrying a heavy current can result in ticking, tiny electrical discharges that can ignite a coating that needs little to get it burning.

Often during maintenance inspections, the technician will see this build-up on the wire bundles and will try to remove it while feeling along the wires for cracks or splits. Sometimes though this very activity can cause cracking and splitting, possibly in wires buried deep in the bundle unseen by the technician. This is more likely to occur, of course, in wiring that is old and brittle. The wire in most airliners is, by rule of thumb, supposed to last for about sixty thousand hours before it is considered ready for replacement. The wiring on TWA Flight 800, for instance, had ninety-six thousand hours on it when the aircraft exploded over the Atlantic—well over 50 percent beyond its design specifications. And wiring is suspected as the trigger that detonated fuel vapour in the large internal gas tank.

Why does a wire continue to burn or to support current when its own metal core—the conductor—is severed? The reason for this is a quirk of the chemical makeup of the insulation on Kapton wiring. It does a fine job of insulating as long as it remains in its original condition; however, once the insulation is burned, its chemical properties change. The Aromatic Polyamide Tape—the very material meant to insulate the hard, metal, current-supporting wire inside—changes chemically to a carbon-based molecule that now conducts electricity (called "flashover" or "arcing"). Then, due to the tremendous temperatures generated by the burning insulation, adjacent bundles of wires in the harness ignite, which, though flame resistant, cannot thwart the intense temperatures. The rest of the insulation, exceeding its temperature tolerance due to the incredible flashover temperatures, will now burn freely. Try as they will to use cost-effective, fire-retardant materials in aircraft, something generating the high temperatures that Kapton does will ultimately defeat any flame-resistant material. In fact most materials will become fuel for the inevitable fire, if it is in close proximity to the heat source.

In more than one in-flight fire, moisture or water dripping on a wire bundle below a toilet has started the process of arcing. An Air Canada flight in June of 1983 diverted and landed at Cleveland airport when an electrical motor shorted out due to cable breakdown. The arcing kept tripping the circuit breaker on the flight deck, which the flight crew kept shoving back in—even held in—until, fortunately, they became occupied with getting their burning DC-9 on the ground. By then the damage had been done. The flight crew had been completely unaware that they were committing the cardinal sin of aiding Kapton wire in its flashover properties. Thirty-six people died in that incident.

Even the aircraft's hull is not immune to such temperatures. The thickness from the outer hull to the inside of the cabin in most modern airliners is about 8 or 10 cm (3 or 4 in.). The hull is painted inside with a corrosion-resistant paint before the wiring is added. Inward from the wiring harnesses is a vapour barrier, and usually a soundproofing material covered by Styrofoam, and finally, the cosmetic plastic interior familiar to any air traveller. Everything is crammed together to conserve space for the passengers. All of this material will burn if exposed to high enough temperatures, or at the very least give off poisonous gases, which in many airliner fires have proved to be more harmful to the passengers than the actual fire. A localized fire in one area of the aircraft can emit fumes that will be carried throughout the entire passenger compartment, either rendering the passengers and crew unconscious or killing them.

There have been many media images depicting the partially burned out hull of an airliner on the tarmac, and it's reasonable for the viewer to think that the metal hull of the airliner melted because of the heat generated by the interior combustibles, such as fuel. This is not necessarily the case, however. Most airliner hulls can burn on their own without help from internal fuelling. The magnesium content that helps to harden and stiffen aluminum also helps it to burn, which is why foam, not water, is used to quell fires on airplanes. Other than the fact that water might exacerbate any electrical problems, the foam coats the aluminum, smothering the output of oxygen from magnesium combustion, which feeds off the oxygen molecules in water. The foam is also non-conductive, preventing electrical arcing in any voltage busses that might still be live.

When a hull is breached by fire, another agent is eagerly waiting to aid the destructive process. This is the airliner's own slipstream, which will generate a pressure-backed oxygenated environment that feeds the fire, driving it like an acetylene torch. The atmosphere inside the pressurized hull rushing out to a lower pressure will accomplish much the same thing. Either way, fire aboard a moving aircraft is a deadly combination.

After the Kapton fire on the Air Canada DC-9, the American and Canadian military—since their aircraft were also Kapton wired—issued a memo recommending that affected aircraft have all volatile cable removed before returning to service. This was accomplished for the most part, by the early 1990s. Though the military took heed of the inherent dangers of Kapton wire, the manufacturers of the world's airliners—Lockheed, Boeing, and McDonnell Douglas—did not. Even NASA's space shuttles were not immune to the scourge of Kapton wiring; late in 1999 they were grounded for inspection and possible replacement of this wiring. Still, some major builders continued to use the wire until the early nineties. One of the last airliners designed and constructed by McDonnell Douglas was a stretch version of the DC-10, re-designated the MD-11. One of those was registered to Swissair with the Swiss designation HB-IWF, the same aircraft that, on the night of September 2, 1998, was assigned to an overseas haul as Swissair Flight 111. So far, the TSB has not addressed the problem of Kapton in commercial aircraft.

Testing the Fire Theory

Since the FDR contained no data on the last six minutes before impact, investigators of the Swissair crash needed to find alternative ways of determining how and why the fire in the cockpit disabled the flight instruments, the CVR, the FDR, and possibly the flight controls.

Evidence of scorching and searing on the aluminum hull above the cockpit provided a major clue; it suggests that a fire in the ceiling of the cockpit, possibly fed by ruptured oxygen lines, burnt through overhead between the cosmetic inner ceiling liner, the sound and heat insulation, and the outer hull, weakening the skin of the outer hull enough for outside air to penetrate, fanning the fire with winds in excess of 300 knots. This would have exacerbated an already critical situation, not only by degrading the hull's integrity but by causing it to melt and tear off in small sections. To determine if this theory was supportable, the TSB investigators had to recreate the conditions and simulate the circumstances involved with the high temperatures apparently endured by the aluminum. They had to determine how much heat would produce the same color, scorching, and searing on the aluminum. They would also have to simulate some of the other conditions that occurred, including the immersion of the metal into cold salt water.

There was another factor to consider: the age and condition of the metal. Aluminum has proven to be a boon to the aviation industry because it is long lasting. Cargo and private aircraft built over fifty years ago are still flying today, producing revenue for their owners. But there are many different types of aviation-grade aluminum, used in varying degrees of thickness and layers. These different grades have a life expectancy dependent on exposure to the elements and on the stresses placed upon them. To some extent, heat is generated by the engines or the aircraft's speed, but at very tolerable temperatures. Other stresses—such as the constant pressurization and depressurizing of the hull—put demands on the aircraft's skin during each and every flight.

There are two famous instances where pressurization caused the failure of the aircraft's skin. The first occurred in the 1950s, when three DeHavilland Comets came apart in the air. The first passenger jet and front-runner in the field was grounded when it could not be determined what caused the crashes. After painstaking experiments, the DeHavilland company discovered that the rivets holding the aluminum plates together were improperly drilled and spaced, causing the skin to tear around them— the result of fatigued metal. By the time they found the solution, the Comet had lost ground to Boeing's 707 and that company never looked back.

But later on, Boeing had problems of its own. In the 1980s, a Boeing 737 flying out of Honolulu lost 6 m (19 ft) off the top of the passenger cabin, directly behind the cockpit. Several passengers were injured, and a flight attendant was killed when she was sucked out of the airplane. To everyone's astonishment, the 737 landed safely. In this case, the aluminum had corroded and failed due to constant stretching and relaxing during the pressurization process.

In an attempt to match the metal's history as closely as possible, the TSB investigators sent samples of the scorched metals, along with unaffected metal of the same type and thickness from elsewhere on Flight 111's airframe to the labs in Ottawa. There, the unaffected metals were exposed to varying degrees of heat and then quenched in salt water. Each time careful analysis was made of the both the original fire-damaged metals and the simulated metals in order to determine a match color and damage. In this way investigators were able to determine what temperatures would cause what damage to a certain thickness and grade of aluminum.

As previously mentioned, it was determined early in the investigation that there must have been severely high heat overhead in the cockpit of the MD-11 because there were indications of molten aluminum and plastic on the floor and on the jump seat. Temperatures in excess of 590°C (1,100°F) were determined to have caused the aluminum to liquefy and splatter in such a manner.

Regardless of what piece of equipment—an overhead light, an entertainment system—triggered it, in the final analysis it was fire, caused by damaged wiring, that killed the passengers and crew of Flight 111.

CHAPTER SIX

Electrical Breakdown

Except for flight and engine controls, all other equipment stopped functioning within seconds on Swissair Flight 111. Although the reasons are still under investigation, this does not prevent us from speculating—as does the TSB—on why such a devastating loss of power occurred. When there is a loss of power to the aircraft lighting, the washrooms, ovens, inflight entertainment systems, etc., it follows that there is a loss of power to all vital equipment on the aircraft. This includes flight instruments, communications, aircraft identifiers, collision-avoidance equipment, navigation equipment, FDR and CVR, and—in the case of some of the newest airliners—the loss of flight and engine controls. That is because there is no discrete power source—or discrete power delivery system to the specific equipment required to fly the aircraft.

To understand how the power is generated and distributed by the three alternators mounted on each of the three MD-11 engines would require an electrical engineering degree and a thorough understanding of the technology that makes up power grids on an MD-11. Nonetheless, we can look at the basics to get a general idea of how power is distributed in order to better grasp the impact of its failure.

Every electrical pathway—wire, circuit, etc.—resists the flow of current to some degree; the longer the pathway, the greater the resistance. When resistance occurs, less voltage gets to the intended piece of equipment. If you try to push too high a current through a narrow gauge wire, the resistance of that wire will convert the excess to heat. When the heat gets too high, the wire will melt. If one wire melts in a bundle (the aircraft industry calls these "harnesses") there is a chance it might damage another wire or several others along with it. So, to compensate, heavy gauge wire is used when voltage is being shunted a long distance. The greater the distance, the larger the gauge of the wire.

Some wires are designed not to melt when they are super heated, but to glow red to white hot. For instance, toasters, heaters, and electric stove elements are designed to glow red hot. White hot is used in light bulbs. Although the same kind of wires are desirable in some applications on an airplane, they cannot be included in a bundle of wires. A melted wire could short circuit, or catch fire and feed on its own insulation. A short circuit can also result if high voltages and currents get into wiring not capable of handling them.

As mentioned in the previous chapter, the wiring in the MD-11 probably contributed to its own failure due to its chemical makeup. To lighten the weight of the wiring in the MD-11, McDonnell Douglas used a new type of insulated electrical conductor: Kapton. This wire, manufactured by DuPont saved about 730 kg (1,600 lbs) in the empty weight of the McDonnell Douglas MD-11. That translates directly into dollars saved; if you save weight in one place, you leave room for additional fuel or additional seats for passengers, and hence more revenue for the airline. However, Kapton wiring, as we have seen, reacts differently to the usual procedures carried out by pilots when they experience a popped circuit breaker, electrical failure, or fire due to some electrical source.

In order to get the necessary voltages from the generating source to the equipment, which in some cases are several hundred feet away, the aircraft industry uses singular, heavy cables to carry the voltage to a voltage bus located close to the equipment. A bus is a heavy gauge electrical cable supplying voltage to a desired location in the aircraft, preferably one close to the equipment it serves. In some cases the bus is a copper, aluminum, or silver bar or tube. A bus is mounted on standoff insulators away from the airframe and any other hazardous material, and distributes power to whatever lighter cable connects to it. In most airliners these busses are located in the equipment bay, just below the cockpit. From there, lesser-gauge wires feed voltage to minor voltage busses in the instrument panel, the overhead panels, and anywhere else that power is required.

Imagine a great river flowing from a huge lake that splits into many different rivulets in a delta. The river is the main bus while the rivulets are the smaller cables feeding the equipment from the bus. The lake is the heavy gauge cable feeding the bus with the maximum pressure of current required to provide all the equipment's needs. If for some reason the cable loses its capability to resist the current, the river overflows its banks; that is, the current escapes its wire and insulation.

To prevent the wire from overheating in the first place, electronics has invented a sacrificial lamb of sorts, called a fuse. A fuse inserted into the electrical path of a certain gauge wire capable of handling a particular current will blow or pop well before the wire begins to react to the effects of too much current going through it. We are all aware of fuses and how they work. They are everywhere from the household wall plug to our workplace processors. Airplanes are no different.

Airplanes use circuit breakers, a heat-sensitive fuse that can be re-activated. Sometimes these are the push-in type that when popped out need only to be pushed back in. Another type is a toggle switch that flips over to "Off" when it blows. Circuit breakers (CBs) work on a very simple principle: When too much current is being fed to (or demanded by) the piece of equipment the CB is protecting, a strip of the conducting metal in the circuit breaker heats up and expands, causing it to lengthen. It is designed to expand in only one direction, causing the resulting "hump" to press against an insulated piston, which in turn opens a switch, thereby cutting the current to the original piece of conducting metal. This all happens in a fraction of a second. Shortly afterwards the strip of metal cools and shrinks, allowing the switch to be depressed, re-energizing the circuit once more.

CBs are everywhere in an aircraft. They are on the main busses, the low-level bus feeds, the equipment power supplied from the low-level feeds, and even internally in the equipment itself. The abundance of fuses enables an operator to isolate any one piece of equipment from the bus or any section of equipment from a bus, or any low-level bus from the main bus. Even the main busses can be isolated from the voltage source in case of a runaway voltage situation.

As mentioned, the voltage source for any bus in an airplane starts at the generator mounted on the engine. In older airplanes these were called generators. In newer airplanes they are called alternators because of the different method they use to produce electricity. Geared to the compressor spool in the engine, these generators—in this case three of them, one on each MD-11 engine—produce current, which is transferred from that source via a heavy gauge conduit to the banks of batteries in the equipment bays in the MD-11's nose. These banks of batteries feed the three main busses, each separate from the other. From there, voltage is disseminated throughout the aircraft.

The modern jetliner is like a little airborne village inhabited by hundreds of people. There is about 270 km of wire in the MD-11 running throughout the aircraft to tend to the passengers' needs: heating, lighting, air conditioning, seat adjustments, toilets, entertainment, and cell phones. Except when the flight attendants are using microwave and electric ovens, by far the most demanding user of current is the cockpit and its myriad flight instruments, communications equipment, weather radar, collision-avoidance systems, tracking equipment, flight control and management systems, computers, thermal measuring sensors, engine monitoring devices, and navigation equipment. Fully one-third of the wire in these aircraft is running between the equipment bay and the flight deck, and all of the aircraft's electrical systems are usually under the management of only two people: the pilot and the first officer. Between them they monitor and control more electrical equipment and wiring than is found in a modern one hundred-unit apartment building.

What is odd about the loss of power on Swissair Flight 111 is that there is reason to believe that all three main voltage busses failed. Something occurred to make three sources of power fed from three different electrical generators to three banks of batteries that fed three main voltage busses *all fail*, apparently simultaneously. As a result, everything run by electricity, (except some emergency equipment which is supposed to be backed up by separate and smaller power reserves, such as batteries) ceased to function. All of the flight instrumentation, the communications equipment, the navigation equipment, and the emergency recording equipment failed. Even the electrical fuel pump to engine number two—situated the whole length of the plane away from the voltage busses in the cockpit—failed. It is fairly certain that the original problem occurred in the newly installed entertainment equipment, just aft of the flight deck bulkhead or in the overhead map light. Given the volatile nature of Kapton wiring, it is entirely possible that a surge or break in one bundle could have taken out all three voltage busses. Once there is fire in one bundle, Kapton's propensity to arc, burn and cascade means that every wire or cable is at risk.

For whatever reason, a piece of equipment used to provide entertainment to the passengers (located away from the equipment bay and the cockpit) or an overhead map light managed to take out all three voltage busses, one after the other. Without instrumentation or autopilot

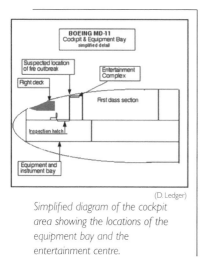

(D. Ledger)

Simplified diagram of the cockpit area showing the locations of the equipment bay and the entertainment centre.

the only means the pilots had to determine whether the aircraft was flying level was by observing the backup Attitude Indicator (AI), supposedly running from a separate battery.

This third AI, a critical piece of instrumentation when flying without any visual reference to the horizon, is located on the MD-11 flight deck, low on the instrument panel just ahead of the centre console and behind the throttle levers. This AI differs from the other two, located in front of the pilots, in that it is a mechanical piece of gyroscopic equipment, driven electrically from a separate battery, whereas the other two AIs are displayed on the instrument panel as images on the CRTs.

(TSB photo)

The so-called "Glass" cockpit of an MD-11. Note the poorly positioned backup Attitude Indicator (AI), (see arrow), low and behind the throttles in the centre console.

The mechanical AI is supposed to have about eighteen minutes running time. It is very possible that it did not. If the electrical system had been disabled by one seemingly harmless harness of wires, or due to some massive voltage surge, caused by a short elsewhere, the battery may have "cooked," rendering it useless. If so, it also malfunctioned, taking away from the pilots the one instrument left that would allow them to maintain level flight; the one instrument vital to the survival of everyone aboard Flight 111.

CHAPTER SEVEN

Flying by the Book

Pilots are good at following procedures, particularly those laid out in the manuals provided by the aircraft manufacturer. Once Zimmermann realized that he was losing circuit breakers, he knew precisely which procedure to follow. He had smoke, but no fire, yet, aboard his aircraft. What had to be particularly disconcerting was that the smoke, and possibly fire, was seemingly there on the flight deck with them.

Sometimes a popped CB will indicate the trouble area, making it easier to isolate. It may be that one piece of equipment's CB will pop a main CB, causing several other equipment CBs to fail at the same time. The pilot then has to determine which is the faulty piece of equipment, usually by the process of elimination. In order to do this, all of the affected CBs are switched off, the main CB is reset and then each piece of equipment is switched back on in sequence. After each reset, there is a brief pause to see if the CB will pop. If it doesn't, the pilot continues resetting until the faulty equipment is isolated.

Of course, pilots don't want to lose several pieces of equipment at once if only one piece is at fault, so they try to isolate the faulty unit, knowing that, for critical functions, they have other equipment to rely on. One of the great things about most aircraft is that more than one instrument will give the same or related information. For instance, an Attitude Indicator will tell the pilot whether the airplane is climbing or diving, banking left or right, or a combination of climbing and banking or diving and banking. There is another piece of equipment called a Turn and Bank (T&B) Indicator, which will tell the pilot the degree of banking and whether it's a turn to the left or right. If the AI should fail, the T&B will provide the information necessary to fly the plane. The Airspeed Indicator (ASI) also indicates whether the plane is climbing or diving (speed falls off in a climb, builds up in a dive), and the Vertical Speed Indicator (VSI or Rate of Climb) will tell how fast the plane is doing this. Incidentally, these three instruments work from air pressure differences and are usually the most reliable of all instruments since there is little about their construction that can fail.

Though this is not the identical model of a Swissair CRT, it shows the general layout of most CRTs in modern airliners. The Airspeed Indicator is on the left, the AI in the middle, the Altitude on the right side, and the Heading Indicator on the bottom.

The aerospace industry has worked to take the guesswork out of instrument reading, particularly in passenger jets, providing the pilots with CRT screens that have colorful images and that eliminate the need for a third crew member in the cockpit. (Installation is a one-time expense rather than paying a third crew member for every flight.) The CRTs provide the same information as the older instruments (popularly known as steam gauges) with all associated markings and information. These steam gauges (their generic hearts still in the equipment bay), are stripped down to the bare essentials. They send their information via an interface and wires to screens on the instrument panel. All of this is accomplished by computers buried in the equipment bay.

The computers' processor takes over many of the chores originally handled by the pilots. It takes the signal provided by mechanical servos and gyros and converts this signal to information and images on the CRT screens. It converts dynamic ram air pressure readings, for instance, into the speed the aircraft is making through the air. Once upon a time this was fed to

More "Glass Cockpit" instrumentation. The weather radar display.

a barometrically driven piece of equipment that was mechanically linked to the needle on the AI dial. Most of the other instruments that used to decorate the instrument panel of the modern airliner are missing in passenger carriers built after 1987 to 1990.

The reason why passengers are asked not to play video games or use a calculator or laptop during takeoff is because of the new low-voltage electronics on the flight deck and in the equipment bay. The latest equipment may be more efficient and accurate, but it is also sensitive. If a heavy voltage-carrying wire were to "bleed" electrical energy through its insulation, into the low voltage and currents of, say, the cockpit computers, then it would play havoc with the delicate circuitry of the computers' processor and memory systems.

The Heading Indicator shows the direction in magnetic degrees in which the aircraft is travelling.

You don't have to go far to find an example of what can happen when a situation like this arises. The NTSB/FBI investigation in the United States of TWA 800 has narrowed the reason for that crash to high-level voltage getting into the low-voltage wiring that passes directly through the massive fuel tank just below and behind the flight deck. These low-voltage cables are incapable of igniting fuel even if they short out, since they only carry data signal rather than voltage. But if a high-level voltage should bleed into or find a circuit through these low-level voltage wires, they will overheat and open, or perhaps arc and flashover. In a near empty fuel tank filled with fumes, the outcome was disastrous.

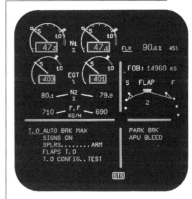

Engine condition display.

Procedures are drilled into pilots from their first tentative flights while getting their private pilot's license. Airline pilots start there, too. There are procedures for fuelling the airplane, and checklists for pre-flight and for run-up of the engine on the tarmac; there are procedures for

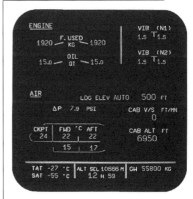

Fuel monitoring system display, cabin altitude pressure, outside air temperatures etc.

contacting Ground Control; for contacting the tower, proceeding to the runway for holding takeoff, and for takeoff itself; there are procedures for entering level flight, for right or left turning, and for turning out to the downwind for a simple rectangular circuit. There are crosswind checks, downwind checks, base-leg checks, and final checks. There are procedures for deploying flaps for dropping gear, and for final approach. There are procedures for getting clearance and landing. All this just to get a light airplane airborne and around a circuit. Multiply this by a hundred and you have some idea of what airline pilots go through to get a 200 to 700 ton aircraft up to altitude and en route to destination.

All of these procedures have been carefully developed and slowly introduced over the span of ninety-seven years, ever since the Wright Brothers made their first flight in 1903. Usually they work. In the case of Flight 111, there is compelling evidence that following procedures did more to bring about the tragic end to Swissair Flight 111 than it did to save it.

Given the number of instruments and their complex wiring on the MD-11 flight deck, Captain Zimmermann did what he had been trained to do: he went with the Standard Operational Procedures (SOPs) laid down by the builders of the MD-11. There are seemingly countless procedures that a pilot should follow during a malfunction of any one of a thousand pieces of equipment. There are several procedure manuals, each inches thick. He knew that there would likely be a dozen or more scenarios and procedures to be followed for the presence of smoke on the flight deck. It was up to him to take his best shot as to where to begin, which depended to some extent on which equipment he thought might be the source of the trouble. First of all, Captain Zimmermann didn't really know what he was dealing with. Co-pilot Loëw had found nothing amiss when he checked the electronics bay. Zimmermann most likely suspected the air conditioning. Air conditioners have been the culprit in a number of flight deck scares, so his first instincts were probably to check this possibility before taking final steps to land the plane: he wouldn't want the company asking him later why he had cost them thousands of dollars on a nonstarter like a smelly air conditioner.

Captain Zimmermann turned to the checklists looking for the proper procedures, while First Officer Loëw flew the plane. The SOPs, in trying to eliminate a problem, naturally also carry safety procedures for the pilots themselves, and the pilots had donned oxygen masks and goggles, which provided emergency breathable atmosphere. The type of oxygen masks and goggles supplied to Flight 111's pilots have long been a source of complaints on many different types of airliners. Whether a full (covering the eyes, nose, and mouth) or partial (covering the nose and mouth) face mask, they all slow down cockpit communications. Voice communication between the pilots on the flight deck then requires an intercom, which is always on and wired to the CVR. A thumb button on the control yoke is used for radio transmissions outside the aircraft. Separate goggles are supposed to accommodate pilots who wear glasses. Since the goggles are not connected to the oxygen source, there is a series of perforations to reduce moisture and minimize fogging. However, vents leave eyes exposed to any smoke and noxious fumes. The eyes can water profusely or accumulated heat can dry the eyes, causing excessive blinking, and impairing a pilot's vision. Captain Zimmermann and First Officer Loëw were wearing masks and goggles presumably because there was sufficient smoke in the cockpit to make them essential. At any rate, it is safe to assume that smoke worsened as the fire progressed, since there is evidence of extremely high temperatures.

The other precaution after assessing the seriousness of the smoke was to make the Pan Pan Pan call to Moncton Center. This allowed Zimmermann to maintain his right to save the flight plan and continue to Geneva should he find and correct the source of the smoke. The situation was not yet an emergency, and he may have thought he could still isolate and correct the problem.

After Moncton suggested Halifax rather than Boston, Zimmermann began a circling manoeuvre to the left, setting the aircraft up for a possible landing at HIA not far away. The GPS would have been telling him—almost to the metre—exactly where Halifax was. The Distance Measuring Equipment (DME) and the inertial guidance were telling him the same thing. So he has three sources giving him the distance and direction to Halifax. A quick call on the radio to Moncton Center could also radar identify the plane, its distance from Halifax and its altitude. Even his radios could be used to get a Direction Finding (DF) fix and steer to Halifax by the controller in Moncton, if all else failed.

When Captain Zimmermann made the Pan Pan Pan call, he was well equipped to land. A simple turn back to the heading into Halifax, a depression of the nose and glide angle, and a reduction of airspeed, would have him over the runways of Halifax International in several minutes. Flying in clear weather over St. Margarets Bay at 8,000 ft he would only have to look downward at about a forty-five-degree angle, past the obscuring nose of the aircraft, to see the airport at Halifax. It appears that close even at a distance of 50 km (30 mi). Zimmermann had to be thinking that he had the runway made, and steering the headings provided by all three instruments would be child's play. He could not know, nor would he have suspected in his wildest dreams, that he was going to lose, in a matter of seconds, all the safeguards and equipment on which he depended. Such failure was unheard of.

Meanwhile, the CVR was recording the pilots' conversations, the sounds of the various enunciators—such as warbles, horns, and alerts—right up to the moment of the catastrophic power failure about six minutes before the aircraft crashed. As the press release from the Transport Safety Board pointed out, these CVR conversations are restricted by Canadian law to the investigators of the crash and can't be released to the general public. To date, there has not even been a summary of these exchanges released to the media, at least not here in Canada.

Despite the Canadian restrictions, it transpired that some agency, either in the United States or possibly Switzerland, leaked details of the CVR recordings to the *Wall Street Journal* (WSJ) including the mentioned discussion or argument between the two pilots. After their release the CTSB's response was that the statements about the text were out of context, but it did not deny them. Officials seemed to be more concerned with plugging leaks during the investigation than determining whether the *Wall Street* story was accurate. But whoever leaked the transcript chose to leak it to one of the most prestigious newspapers in North America, which is possibly why the CTSB chose not to pursue the matter or vigorously argue the accuracy of the report.

The story implied that there was strong disagreement between First Officer Loëw and Captain Zimmermann about the course of action they should be taking an implication that is, in my view, questionable. Some newspapers chose to interpret this conversation as an "argument," which the CTSB insists is erroneous. As a pilot I would have to agree with the CTSB.

Knowing pilots and how they discipline themselves to follow prescribed procedures, and knowing the strict hierarchy observed on the flight deck, particularly in the European flying community, it is highly unlikely that the co-pilot would actually argue with the captain. He might voice a concern, or suggest an alternative course of action. But he wouldn't argue.

Loëw was an instructor, like Zimmermann, as well as a first officer with one of the world's most prestigious airlines. It's doubtful that he would have gotten that far by being argumentative with his captains.

According to the *Wall Street* story, the flight crew were eating their dinners when the first hint of smoke odour crept in to the flight deck at 10:16 P.M. local time. A couple of minutes later, Captain Zimmermann told First Officer Loëw that he could definitely smell smoke. The two pilots discussed turning the aircraft back to Boston or possibly Bangor, Maine, but since he was now in Moncton Center's sector Captain Zimmermann called his Pan Pan Pan into the controller there.

As we already know from the earlier transcript, in chapter one, the Moncton controller suggested Halifax rather than Boston because it was nearly straight ahead of Flight 111 and had all the necessary facilities for an emergency landing. MD-11 was just over Liverpool, Nova Scotia, about 70 nautical miles (134 km or 80.5 mi) out of Halifax and cruising at about 9 miles a minute. This speed would have put the plane over HIA in about ten minutes.

Had Zimmermann opted to fly directly to HIA, it is possible that this book would never have been written. Perhaps there would have been a heck of a news story about an airliner that landed at Halifax and burned up on the runway after the passengers had left the plane, as was the case in an earlier incident involving an MD-11.

Captain Zimmermann was perhaps unaware that, in that incident, a Fed-Ex cargo carrier declared an emergency over Newburgh, New York, after smoke was discovered aboard the aircraft. The MD-11 landed right away, although in this instance the co-pilot wanted to follow procedures and make a slow descent while going through the checklist. The pilot, however, was having none of it. He descended quickly and immediately, landing as soon as possible. Fed-Ex Flight 1406 burned up on the runway shortly afterward. Its crew of three escaped unharmed. The pilot was a hero. He had made the right decision.

On Flight 111, co-pilot Stephan Loëw, like the captain of Fed-Ex 1406, was apparently having misgivings about following book procedures, suggesting to his captain that a quick descent and landing on Runway 06 at Halifax was the prudent course of action. The *Journal* story suggests he made this suggestion more than once but was rebuffed by the captain, who reportedly told Loëw that he did not want to be disturbed so often.

The *Journal* story also mentions a difference in respiration rates between the two pilots. Zimmermann, ultimately shouldering the responsibility for this flight, was breathing rapidly. His respiration rate, recorded on the CVR from the microphone in his oxygen mask, was at 25 breaths per minute (one inhalation and expiration every 2.4 seconds). This indicates that the captain was stressed but does not suggest that he was panicked. Zimmerman was pumping adrenaline, and was acutely aware of his responsibility to the passengers and his company, as well as his own reputation and possibly his career.

Loëw's respiration rate, on the other hand, was in the more normal range of 11 breaths per minute. He, of course, would not have to make the final decisions; however, he could make suggestions, such as the quick diversion to Halifax. Blame wouldn't fall his head if the reason for the diversion turned out to be trivial.

Loëw may have been right, but—unless a Captain is incapacitated— there are no circumstances under aeronautical law that allow first officers the right to assume command and take control of a situation. Co-pilots have often and repeatedly expressed concerns before finally acquiescing to the captain's authority; in some cases, they have died as a result.

One example where this behavior caused a horrendous accident, resulting in a high loss of life, occurred on March 27,1977, at Tenerife Airport in Spain's Canary Islands. Two of the world's largest airliners were involved. The airfield that day was shrouded in thick fog. A Pan American Boeing 747 was taxiing on the active runway, while another airliner—a Dutch KLM 747—took off without clearance. The KLM plane tore through the cabin roof of the Pan Am 747, which was still on the runway, having just begun a turn onto a taxiway. Between these two aircraft, 582 people were killed, including the KLM's flight crew.

The Tenerife Tower tapes and the KLM-747 CVR tapes clearly indicate that the KLM Captain did not have clearance to take off, and that this was conveyed to him several times by his co-pilot, who was ignored. The co-pilot was told by his Captain that "he's clear" (referring to the Pan Am jet), despite the fact that the tower had not given clearance; the co-pilot acquiesced to his superior—likely justifying this by thinking 'he's the Captain, he probably knows better.'

The KLM Captain was, in fact, the darling of KLM's pilot corp and company, a handsome man regularly used by their ad agencies in promotional material. It would have taken a great deal of courage for that co-pilot to have slapped the Captain's hands from the throttles and pressed stubbornly on the toe-brakes, thus preventing the plane from taking off. After all, neither man could see far enough down the runway to ascertain if there was another aircraft there.

For the want of a half-ounce of pressure on the microphone activation switch on the Captain's control yoke and a terse "Tower, KLM Flight . . . confirm that the runway is clear and that we are cleared for take-off," 582 people lost their lives.

Loëw was likely suffering, to some degree, from the same deeply-ingrained respect for a Captain's authority. Had he decided to take command somehow incapacitate Zimmermann, and then land safely at HIA, he would still have faced a board of inquiry for usurping Zimmermann's command. And he likely would have been censured for it, possibly even lost his job. Airline captains, like their marine counterparts, have a great deal of authority which is not to be trifled with, and the first officers know this. Someone has to make the final decision, and that responsibility and power rests with the captain on the flight deck. There isn't time in most crises situations to put a decision to a vote, and, when there's only two voting, who wins?

According to William M. Carley's report in the *Wall Street Journal*, a summary report of the cockpit recording compiled by the CTSB revealed that the co-pilot preferred a rapid descent. He suggested dumping fuel early so the jet wouldn't be too heavy to land. And he was not in favour of turning out to sea to dump fuel.

However, rather than landing immediately in Halifax, Zimmermann wanted to go through the checklist supplied by the MD-11's manufacturers, abiding by company policy, as years of training had taught him to do. The *Journal* again reports that a source close to the CTSB investigation revealed that at one point on the cockpit recording Capt. Zimmermann—in response to Loëw's advice that they proceed immediately to Halifax—supposedly replied, "Don't bother me, I'm going through the checklist."

The Canadian Transportation Safety Board disputes these interpretations by the *Journal*, claiming, as mentioned, that they are out of context and contrary to the behavior of pilots on an airliner flight deck. Either way, the public will never be able to determine that for themselves. Whatever the case, Zimmermann was apparently confident that in the procedural checklists a solution could be found to what he considered at the time may be a minor problem.

Capt. Urs Zimmermann was, unknowingly, approaching an emergency situation in which he would have only precious seconds to make the right decision. In other words, he had to decide if he was going to err on the side of caution, only to find a non-starter when he got on the ground thereby possibly causing inconvenience and costs to his company, and jeopardizing his standing in the company and among his fellow pilots, or to follow prescribed procedure in order to solve the problem. The lives of 228 other people were in the balance.

Although governing authorities are reluctant to change protocol that has been around for centuries, there has been a gradual move in the airline business to encourage captains to be more open to suggestions from first officers. It's an attempt to eliminate authority clashes, allowing first officers to voice their opinions without fear of retribution. It also allows captains to take suggestions without fear of compromising their authority or professional integrity. No one is more critical of pilots than other pilots. Sometimes the criticism is so harsh that it drives pilots out of the profession.

It should be stressed that over the years, pilots have more than proved their courage attempting to save lives in hazardous situations. But the threat of losing their pilot's license and therefore their livelihood—can sometimes cloud their instincts. In any confrontational situation with their airline, pilots know they are dispensable. All they have is their license, their experience, and their integrity. Take away an airline pilot's license and you not only take away his livelihood but also his reason for living. Most pilots will tell you they are happiest when they have at least ten feet of air under their seats. No one sets out to be an airline captain; they choose to be pilots simply because they love to fly.

It's easy to understand why Zimmermann—with the standing he had in his company and the stake he had in his own future—would choose to go by the book. For all intents and purposes, he was right, although in hindsight he was wrong. On a recent television program, an airline pilot observed, "If you go against the rules and you pull it off, you're a hero, but if you don't, you're a dog." Although it could be argued that Captain Zimmermann made the wrong choice in this case, I've yet to hear one pilot say that he was wrong.

Ironically, if Zimmermann did make the wrong decision it's possible it alone will be responsible for saving many lives in the future. Pilots will now have this tragedy to point to. There will be no hesitation the next time there is evidence of smoke in the cockpit. In fact, ever since the crash, pilots have been slamming "heavies" down on runways by the dozens at the mere hint of smoke anywhere in the aircraft. Hardly a week goes by now that there isn't a report of an airliner making a precautionary or emergency landing due to the presence of smoke or some odour in the airplane.

Once Zimmerman's Pan Pan Pan call was made to Moncton, the pilots' next priority was to turn off all electrical power to the passenger cabins, to effectively eliminate any electrically, caused problems there. If smoke is still evident somewhere in the aircraft, the next procedure is to reconfigure some of the aircraft systems so that various communications and navigation systems can be allocated to alternative sources of electrical power. The transponders and VHF radios are examples of equipment that can be recycled to other voltage busses.

When the systems have been satisfactorily assigned, the next protocol is to recycle the Smoke Elec/Air Switch. This switch, located on the overhead panel between the pilots, requires a push in and turn motion. It has four positions and is kept in the Normal position during a routine flight. It can be set to achieve any number of the several functions. For instance, turning the switch clockwise will disable certain air and electrical systems (or combinations of these) to isolate certain circuits that might be causing smoke.

If one of the three generators fails, moving the switch out of normal mode voltage busses allow the remaining generators to supply voltage to all or some of the circuits supplied by the failed generators. Pilots refer to the operation manual in order to follow the right procedure; it's not the kind of knowledge they would likely have at hand.

The following example, from the respected aerospace magazine *Aviation Week and Space Technology*, written by Dan Dornheim, addresses the problems facing the pilots on Flight 111. It also shows how pressure can mount during a crisis situation, when a pilot is suddenly be called upon to implement complicated procedures, and could explain why Captain Zimmermann didn't want to be distracted:

The first switch position, "3/1 OFF," turns off the aircraft's No. 3 generator channel as well as the systems for bleeding air from the No. 1 engine's compressor and filtering it through the No. 1 air-conditioning system as cabin air. If the smoke dissipates, the crew is to leave the switch in this position. If it does not, the switch is turned to the "2/3 OFF "and "1/2 OFF" positions, which turn off the corresponding electrical and air systems.

The No. 3 electrical system uses the generator on the No. 3 engine to power the No. 3 a.c. bus, the No. 3 d.c. bus and the Right Emergency a.c. and d.c. busses. The No. 3 system provides power to the aircraft's Nos. 2 and 3 VHF radios, the No. 2 transponder and the flight data recorder (FDR). On some aircraft, one of those busses also may power the cockpit voice recorder (CVR).

The checklist calls for the pilots to select another radio and transponder before turning the "Smoke Elec/Air" switch to the "3/1 OFF" position. If for some reason a crew did not do that, the aircraft's radio and transponder would go dead when "3/1 OFF" was selected, as would the FDR and possibly the CVR.

In fact the Mode C transponder, radio communications, FDR and CVR all ceased to function six minutes before Flight 111 crashed. Whether this was due to an improper or inadvertent setting of the "Smoke Elec/Air" switch is not known, but there is no indication on the FDR that Captain Zimmermann or First Officer Loëw did recycle this switch.

To suggest that Zimmermann or Loëw were unfamiliar with the usage of the "Smoke Elec/Air" switch would be unfair. Captain Zimmermann in particular would have no doubt done simulator training for the eventuality of in-flight fire, probably many times during his command of MD-11s. This would not have prevented him from going to the procedures manual if the occasion arose, if for no other reason than he wanted to assure himself that he was correctly recycling the "Smoke Elec/Air" switch. In hindsight, there was little time for following procedures, and it appears that attempting to do so compounded a swiftly-escalating crisis.

One procedure—more than any other—that seems to have influenced Zimmermann's decision not to fly direct to Halifax was that the aircraft was carrying a full load of fuel. According to his manual, at the plane's current weight, the chance of landing safely in Halifax and stopping on a 2,680-m (8,800-ft) runway was marginal. After the crash of Flight 111, Swissair argued that the plane could not have landed safely and cited several unsuccessful simulated attempts to land aircraft under the same altitude and weight condition, even when fuel was being dumped.

At any rate, thirteen months after the crash of Flight 111, in October 1999, in the same area at the same approximate altitude and distance from Halifax International as Flight 111 had been, a Continental Airlines DC-10 (the forerunner of the MD-11), was on a trip to Zurich from New York when one of the male passengers became violent, injuring several of the flight crew and sexually assaulting one of the female flight attendants. The DC-10 was about twenty minutes out of Halifax. The pilot radioed an emergency, dumped fuel during a straight-in approach, and landed safely in Halifax without damage to the aircraft. The passenger was arrested by the RCMP and charged.

Whether Zimmermann chose to dump fuel over the water as a courtesy, or to delay landing until enough fuel had been dumped, is unclear.

But it is a misconception that pilots are obliged to dump fuel in remote areas. At least, this is not true in Canada. Pilots can dump fuel wherever they please during an emergency, and if there was a rule forbidding it, it could be broken with impunity. No pilot is going to concern himself greatly about a little fuel contamination when the lives of passengers are at stake. Any fuel dump above 150 m. is not going to have much of an impact anyway, because fuel tends to atomize very quickly. Aside from the unpleasant smell, very little makes it to the ground.

In addition to possible fuel concerns, Captain Zimmermann also suggested that he wanted time to allow flight attendants to prepare the passengers and cabin for landing. The evening meals had been served and food trolleys were in the aisles between the seats, a dangerous situation for several reasons should the aircraft have to make an emergency landing. First, trolleys would have proved an impediment to flight attendants who'd be moving around the cabin making last-minute emergency arrangements for the passengers and for themselves. Second, these trolleys would become lethal missiles if left unrestrained in the aisles. Third the trolleys would have blocked aisles while passengers were attempting to evacuate.

Again in hindsight, Captain Zimmermann could have been dumping fuel all the way to Halifax International while using any number of procedures to bleed off speed and altitude. There are many ways to circumvent weight and height limitations and still land an aircraft safely. What pilots refer to as bringing an aircraft in "dirty" means making the airplane less aerodynamic or slippery. Dropping the landing gear, putting on flaps, and extending the leading edge slats is one way to slow the airplane down and lose altitude more rapidly, but popping the spoilers is the most efficient. The aircraft goes into a high sink rate while still travelling forward at a good speed when using spoilers. Once closer to an airport the other measures would likely be brought into play. Even forward or side slipping, using the airplane's own side profile as a drag element, can be used to bleed off altitude and speed. As for the weight problem, pilots know that there is some margin of safety built into the numbers and feel it is safe to exceed them, if only by a small percentage. And a lot of fuel could have been pumped overboard in the ten minutes it would have taken Flight 111 to glide down the slope into Halifax International Airport.

For his own reasons, Captain Zimmermann chose to continue his check-list protocol, and turned away from HIA. The aircraft made a wide loop-ing turn to the southwest and then to the south, heading inland from St. Margarets Bay as far as 5 nautical miles before crossing over Queensland. There, Flight 111 levelled out on a heading of 179 degrees that took the plane once more out over St. Margarets Bay, on an almost straight course for Peggys Light. For fourteen more seconds they maintained this heading, when suddenly the autopilot warbler alarm activated, and Zimmermann informed Moncton Center at 10:24:28.1 local, "we must fly manually." Eighteen seconds later, both pilots scrambled to declare an emergency. Ten seconds after that Zimmermann declares that the aircraft has to "land im-mediate." By now Zimmermann had no doubt abandoned any attempt to continue with a checklist procedure as things were coming to a head on the flight deck. The warbler warning that the autopilot had disconnected continued to enunciate and, according to the FDR, the flight control com-puter and some other systems were going off-line.

In the few seconds remaining before loss of contact, Zimmermann continued to converse with the controller at Moncton Center about dump-ing fuel, and, strangely, the controller continued to give him instructions, even though an emergency had been declared and the pilot no longer needed to clear anything with Moncton Centre. And Zimmermann stead-fastly maintained a southeasterly heading of 179 degrees magnetic, still not turning back toward HIA. Every ten seconds took Flight 111 1.6 km (1 mi.) further to the southeast while HIA was off to the northwest.

Then, quite suddenly, everything except the engines and manual con-trols failed on Flight 111. Captain Zimmermann and First Officer Loëw were on their own with no contact with the outside world. To make mat-ters worse, a low cloud cover was obscuring their vision so they had no way of knowing where they were or their angle of flight. The last strike against them was the weather.

CHAPTER EIGHT

The Weather

When private pilot Grant Kennedy flew over the mouth of St. Margarets Bay on the night of September 2, 1998, on a course that would land him fifteen minutes later at CFB Shearwater, he had no idea of the drama that was about to unfold behind him. Grant, a sound engineer with Atlantic Television (ATV) in Halifax, was returning from Yarmouth Airport on the southwestern tip of Nova Scotia. He had flown his Grumman Tiger AA5B through marginal weather all the way to Shearwater, at most times in between cloud layers with little reference to ground details. In fact, he flew through the same weather that Flight 111 would encounter just several kilometres south of Grant's flight path.

Grant's aircraft's cruise was about 145 mph, as opposed to Swissair Flight 111's approximate 600 mph, which meant that the MD-11 was catching up fast, arriving over Liverpool, Nova Scotia, and re-contacting Moncton Center just about the time Grant was touching down at CFB Shearwater.

Grant's observations about the local weather while inbound for Shearwater are of interest here, because they give a first-hand account of conditions near the crash site. They also provide an idea of what the flight crew of Flight 111 would have been experiencing once they lost their navigational and aircraft situational equipment at 10:25:41 P.M. local time. Earlier I suggested that there were four factors that contributed to the crash of Flight 111. The weather was the final straw in the Swissair tragedy on September 2. Minutes before the crash, Zimmermann had reported to the Halifax control tower that he had to fly manually, indicating that he had lost all of his navigation aids. Whether he intended to try to make it back to Halifax, now 15 minutes away, or to crash into the

Atlantic is not known. What we do know is that, either way, without instrumentation, he needed a reference point to the ground in order to keep his plane level and horizontal.

I am almost certain that, after all of their trials and tribulations, the crew on Flight 111 lost their reference to the horizon and crashed, inverted, into the Atlantic as a result. I've flown over St. Margarets Bay many times on my own, and I'm very familiar with that area. The flight I would make with Grant was the first time that I'd flown over the area at night. The purpose of this flight was to familiarize myself with what the Flight 111 pilots would have seen on that September night.

As mentioned, the MD-11 had three separate instruments to ensure that its pilots would have critical information regarding the aircraft's flight. Given its angle of entry into the water, all three must have failed. To understand how this could have happened requires another look at Kapton wiring. The initial cause of this chain of events that resulted in the devastating impact of Flight 111 into the waters off Peggys Cove might have been present several days or even years before the event. Most likely it can be traced back to the installation of the Kapton wiring into the airframe of the MD-11 when it was built in 1990-91. Any number of things could have occurred during the installation that might have eventually caused the Kapton wiring to break down and cause a fire. In the flying game, seemingly unimportant occurrences suddenly become critical when the unforeseeable happens.

For instance, more than one airplane has crashed because a panel light came on or failed to come on when it was supposed to. An airliner inbound into Miami crashed into a Florida swamp while the pilot and co-pilot fiddled with a faulty indicator light on the instrument panel. Each time they leaned forward to adjust it, they bumped the control column forward which disengaged the autopilot; and, each time, the aircraft incrementally lost altitude until it pancaked into a swamp, broke up and exploded, killing half the passengers on impact while the other half waited for rescue in alligator-infested waters, some dying as a result.

Cargo is another seemingly minor factor. But improper stowage of cargo in an aircraft can cause disaster when cargo shifts, affecting the airplane's centre of gravity (C of G) and trim. Fuel management on some aircraft is critical for the same reason and must be shunted around via fuel lines in order to maintain the aircraft's equilibrium. An aircraft's C of G is important because it has a great deal to do with the airplane's natural stability. Usually being weighted forward is more desirable than weighted aft. If an airplane is slightly weighted forward, meaning it has a nose down tendency, it can be trimmed to keep it flying straight and level. Neutralizing the trim will allow the aircraft to drop its nose and build up speed, creating more airflow over the control surfaces, thus giving the pilot more control. Tail heavy, on the other hand, is much less desirable. It, too, can be trimmed out but if, for some reason, that trim is lost, then the aircraft wants to sink tail first—a direction that allows no airflow over the control surfaces, at least not in the right direction—resulting in loss of control. The aircraft will tend to go into a flat spin that is usually not correctable in an airliner or in most other aircraft.

The MD-11 is one of the few aircraft that carries fuel in its horizontal stabilizers, the little wings on the back of the airplane. The reason is that engine No. 2 requires a constant source of fuel that can be shunted between the main wings and the horizontal stabilizers, to maintain that all-important trim, and also as a reserve, acting as a sort of header tank from which the electric fuel pump can draw jet fuel from a short distance rather than from the main tanks nearly 35 m (115 ft) away.

According to the Transport Safety Board, engine No. 2 quit because of a loss of power to its fuel pump. That means that it was not sucking fuel from the tail wing tanks. Since there was no power, fuel could not be shunted forward by electric pumps from the tail wing tanks to counteract the tendency of tail heaviness. To make matters worse, fuel was being dumped from the forward tanks to lighten the aircraft, which would have had a slight tendency to buoy the nose up rather than to make the airplane slightly 'nose heavy.' If pilots have lost all references to the horizon, it would be helpful if the plane were to stay level on its own, rather than mushing through the air with the nose high. That way, the pilot has a chance to attend to other things without worrying about whether the plane is flying straight and level. So there are two problems in the MD-11, both of which were built into the aircraft with good intentions. First, the Kapton wiring is lighter than its counterparts but subject to arcing; second, a lighter pump draws fuel from the tail wings but makes the plane tail-heavy.

Another MD-11 problem is the positioning of the backup AI, mounted low behind the throttle levers and in the centre on the instrument panel. This instrument has been highlighted by some MD-11 pilots for its very awkward location as a reference for level flight. As mentioned earlier, in the event of total electrical failure, the backup AI is supposed to operate up to eighteen minutes from its own separate battery, which is recharged

periodically from the main power busses. But if this battery for some reason does not hold a charge, then it is not going to do its job. Presumably
there is a warning device in the aircraft to alert maintenance crews to the
integrity of the battery during regular maintenance checks, and some
alerting mechanism for the pilots, should this valuable backup system fail
in flight.

In addition to an inboard Kapton fire, an unstable aircraft, and the
awkward location of a critical instrument control, Flight 111's pilots were
also encumbered by awkward emergency equipment (face masks) that most
likely was not protecting their eyes in a smoky environment, while trying
to communicate with one another through an intercom system that, like
everything else, had suddenly gone dead. If these conditions weren't bad
enough, the visibility on the other side of the windscreen certainly was.

Because Grant Kennedy had first-hand experience with the weather
the night of September 2, 1998, I asked him to take me out over the St.
Margarets Bay area, so I could get a sense of what the Swissair pilots may
have experienced that night. Besides, I had a theory about why
Zimmermann made the convoluted flight that we were about to retrace.
Kennedy readily agreed to take me. Within a couple of days we were
ready to overfly the route taken by Flight 111, using the track provided
by the TSB on their Web site. Since the track was drawn on a Canadian
VFR navigation chart (VNC), we had an accurate scale of reference.

On the night of October 11, 1999, Grant, myself, and Gary Theriault—
the manager of the Shearwater Flying Club—lifted off from CFB
Shearwater at 7:20 P.M. local, in the same Grumman Tiger that Grant was
flying the night of the crash. We took a left-hand turnout off Runway 34
and flew over Halifax Harbour to the Halifax peninsula. Once over the
peninsula we took a slightly southwesterly heading toward the Atlantic
Ocean. This took us to a point over the Head of Prospect Bay where Grant
turned the Grumman onto the track flown by Flight 111.

On my right was the city of Halifax sprawled out to the northeast.
The lights spread almost to the horizon, sprinkled around the basin at the
north end of the harbour, then out toward Sackville and back around to
Dartmouth on its opposite shore in a big, illuminated horseshoe. Much
further off to my right, northeast of Dartmouth, the lights on the end of
Runway 06 at Halifax International Airport were clearly visible. When
we reached the intersection of highways 103 and 213 we banked—as Flight
111 had done—around to the left on a course that would take us the few
kilometres southwest, to Queensland Beach. Once there, we turned again

to the left on a southeasterly heading. We were now on a heading toward Indian Harbour and the flashing beacon at Peggys Cove, still following the track taken by Flight 111.

The weather on this particular evening differed from that of September 2, 1998; it was absolutely beautiful and clear, despite the fact that the weather had been marginal a few hours before. A pilot usually wishes for good weather to fly in and more often than not gets bad; this night I was hoping for at least some cloud cover, and got perfectly clear skies instead.

Grant gave me a detailed description of the weather—particularly in the St. Margarets Bay area, Blandford, and Peggys Cove: on the night of the crash. He recalled a low cloud layer at about 2,000 ft, blanketing St. Margarets Bay and vicinity. The controller at Terminal Control had brought him down to as low a level as possible, which was 2,100 ft and the cloud layer was just below him. High above, at 12,000 and 17,000 ft were other thin layers of cloud, but they were of no concern to him since, without oxygen, he was restricted to levels below 10,000 ft. We knew that by the time the search got underway on the night of September 2, winds were out of the east to northeast, off the Atlantic, blowing sometimes as much as 30 to 35 knots, fog patches and drizzle—even reports of localized hail showers over St. Margarets Bay—but that Halifax skies were relatively clear.

I was curious to know how well Halifax would have shown up in the pilot's windscreen on that night from their positions over St. Margarets Bay. We were only at an altitude of about 5,000 ft, compared to Flight 111's 10,000 ft, and we could clearly see the surrounding area. For instance, even at our altitude the lights of the city of Halifax on the opposite side of the Halifax peninsula were plainly visible and distinct under our left wing. It was easy to see the two suspension bridges spanning the harbour between Halifax and Dartmouth, the lights of Dartmouth, and individually lit streets in both cities.

As mentioned, we could easily see the end of Runway 06 at Halifax International Airport 47 km (28 mi) away, even with the lights at low intensity. I've approached HIA at night when the lights were at high intensity, and they are almost blinding. Had the weather been clearer on the night of September 2, 1998, things might have gone quite differently for Flight 111. HIA would have been right there as a visual reference to the northeast of the city. The pilots would have plainly seen the welcoming lights of Runway 06. The tragedy is that if they had just turned toward Halifax while they still had their navigation and IFR instruments, they would have run out of the low cloud layer. Halifax would have been there in the open, and the plane could have been landed manually using visual references.

Grant noted that there were a few breaks in the cloud that night. He had infrequent glimpses of Peggys Light and other lighted features on the ground. The lights he recalled seeing on the southern end of the Aspotogan Peninsula were likely the floodlights at the fish processing plant in New Harbour, at the peninsula's southernmost tip. These same floodlights, highly visible from many kilometres away, were illuminated the night of my flight with Grant.

To the northwest he could see a dull orange glow from the lights of Halifax and Dartmouth illuminating the clouds from below, but there was no visible detail. This orange glow, Grant noted, obscured any hint of the lights at Halifax International about 19 km (12 mi) beyond the north-eastern boundary of Halifax. For the record, it's about 27 nautical miles (about 52 km) from Peggys Cove to the button of Runway 06-24 at HIA. By automobile that is about a one-hour drive. Aboard Flight 111 the trip would have taken less than four minutes.

Suddenly, all the pieces to my theory came together. Yes, I thought, that must be it...Zimmermann was flying blind! Geographically, he didn't know where he was, otherwise he would have turned back toward Halifax Airport; and, specifically, he didn't know his angle of flight, and couldn't know it without a reference point to the ground. Momentarily, he glimpsed through the clouds, as Grant had done that night, the flashing light of the beacon at Peggys Cove, or the flood lights of the fishing plant at New Harbour. His convoluted flight was an effort to use one or the other to give him the reference he so desperately needed. And then the cloud cover, pushed by 35 knot winds and heavy with rain or hail, moved in, obscuring his vision, and depriving him of his last hope even for a crash landing. That was why Swissair entered the unforgiving waters of St. Margarets Bay, nose-down and inverted.

Grant made a spiralling turn out around the Little and Big Tancook Islands, then turned sharply back in over the Aspotogan Peninsula and flew over Blandford and Bayswater Beach, as Flight 111 had done, but we stopped short of flying to the restricted airspace over the impact site. It was marked even then by a small vessel guarding the site, which remained restricted for a few more weeks. We chose only to look and remember, passing the area on our way back to Shearwater.

We landed at 8:00 P.M. local and taxied back to the Flying Club. When we reached the expansive concrete Tarmac, where all light aircraft are tied down in front of the Flying Club and its hangar, the moon was shining in a field of stars. On our right, 30 m away, we passed Hangar A, the final resting place of Swissair Flight 111.

Grant taxied to his tie-down area, did a mag check, then shut the engine down. We pushed the pretty little Grumman back into her slot. I looked over toward Hangar A. The lights were on inside. I wondered if they were still working away at the puzzle that constituted the remains of Flight 111. Then I followed Grant and Gary through the hangar doors into the Flying Club. Inside, a dozen people were grouped around a Cessna 172. One of them was pointing out details on the airplane.

New student pilots. About twenty had signed up in the last few weeks. The mausoleum across the way, Hangar A, didn't seem to deter them. That was good. If anything, according to Gary, there has been an increase in student enrollment since the Swissair crash.

I walked past a recently restored Grumman Banshee, an older model jet that flew off our aircraft carriers when the navy had them. Behind that was a Harvard, freshly painted in its famous glossy yellow. It was reflecting the lights hanging from the girders above, waiting to go on display. It's hard to imagine how one can love a big chunk of metal like that . . . but pilots do.

CHAPTER NINE

The Last Six Minutes

Just as Flight 111 was crossing over Queensland Beach at 10:24:42 P.M. (see flight track, p.134, no.8) local time, things began to go terribly wrong aboard the Swiss airliner. The plane was at an altitude of 10,200 ft on a magnetic heading of 179 degrees, a course that would take it directly toward Peggys Light, whether by accident or design. Suddenly the controller at Moncton heard a quick message from Captain Zimmermann. "Swissair one-eleven heavy is declaring emergency." There was an overlapping transmission from First Officer Loëw to the same effect, followed by Zimmermann continuing with, "Roger, we are between 12,000 and 5,000 ft. We are declaring emergency now at, time, zero-one-two-four."

This was a telling transmission, not only because of its urgency but because it indicates that Captain Zimmermann wasn't sure what his altitude was. Although he claimed to be between 12,000 ft and 5,000 ft—a discrepancy of 7,000 ft—the FDR indicates the aircraft was at an altitude of 10,200 ft. Moreover, the flight control computer was failing, the autopilot had already inexplicably disconnected once, and the CRT displays on the instrument panel had gradually winked out. Slowly but surely Flight 111 was going blind.

The Moncton Controller responded with a terse "Roger," the universal response that pilots and controllers use to signify they understood the last transmission. A few seconds passed then Zimmermann informed Moncton Center that he was starting his fuel dump and that he had to "land immediate."

For whatever reason, four seconds later the controller at Moncton Center responded with, "Swissair one-eleven, just a couple of miles, I'll be right with you." A couple of miles to where, one wonders. To the dump site? Captain Zimmermann politely rogered the controller's transmission over the sound of the autopilot disconnect warbler. Then suddenly and for the second time both pilots were attempting to transmit at the same time, both declaring an emergency and stating that they must land immediately. This was possibly in reaction to a new emergency in the cockpit, or to reiterate the emergency after the Moncton controller's oblique response. The FDR picks up indications of continuing disruptions in systems services and in some cases total shutdown of equipment.

The Moncton controller's passive response to the emergency transmission suggests that Moncton Centre didn't actually get Zimmerman's message; at any rate he repeats, "And we are declaring emergency now, Swissair one-eleven."

The controller responds with a terse "Copy that." A full 11 seconds elapses before the controller transmits again with the redundant statement, "Swissair one-eleven, you are cleared to commence your fuel dump on that track and advise me when the dump is complete." Zimmermann didn't need the controller's permission; and he was probably already dumping fuel. Not having received a reply to the last transmission, the Halifax controller in Moncton repeated, "Swissair one-eleven, check you're cleared to start the fuel dump."

Still receiving no response, the Moncton controller transmits again, "Swissair one-eleven, check you're cleared to start the fuel dump." A tense six seconds went by. Then at 10:25:49 P.M. a faint, unintelligible transmission came back from Flight 111, even though the FDR had ceased to record eight seconds before. (See flight track, p.134, no.8).0 Shortly after, the aircraft's transponder signal was lost. Still, Swissair managed to stay flying: Halifax radar continued to paint the jet on their radar scopes, and 100 km away at CFB Greenwood, the flight was also being observed and plotted on radar.

Flight 111 continued on the same heading of 179 degrees at an altitude of 10,200 ft and a speed of 318 knots (610 kph) halfway to the mouth of St. Margarets Bay on a course that took it almost over Indian Harbour and just west of Peggys Cove. The Halifax controller in Moncton tried repeatedly to contact Flight 111 without success. It remained out of contact for the rest of its short and tragic flight.

Swissair Flight 111 was on its own. What follows is both fact and conjecture about what might have happened during those last six minutes, pieced together from the best available information.

At 10:26:04 P.M. local time, Flight 111 was crossing over Shut-In Island at an altitude of 10,000 ft and still flying perfectly when radar suddenly lost its transponder signal. (See flight track, p.134, no.10). It continued on its track of 179 degrees for several seconds then began a gentle turn to the right over Paddys Head and Yowler's Light. Twenty seconds before it was to reach Peggys Cove—the site that would become the marker for its eventual resting place—the Swissair jet began describing a giant backward figure six that would take some 58 km (36 mi) to complete.

On the flight deck of Flight 111, Zimmermann and Loëw were unaware they still had a chance of making a landing at Halifax International Airport. Had they instead swung the yoke on the control column to the left, banked the aircraft around 130 degrees, and headed to the northeast, the pilots would have overflown the low cloud layer that was probably impeding their sight, and would have seen the high-intensity lights of Runway 06-24 laid out before them on a nearly straight-in approach. Since they knew their direction of flight just before the failure of their instruments, it would have been simple enough then to change their course in the direction of Halifax International Airport. Their first turn away from Halifax International Airport was to dump fuel, but why they chose to turn their aircraft away a second time is open to conjecture.

No doubt Captain Zimmermann and First Officer Loëw were distracted and unnerved by serious, and possibly life-threatening, events that were unfolding on their flight deck. Fire had most likely broken out in earnest, probably having spread into the cockpit ceiling from further back, behind the after bulkhead. Smoke on the flight deck was thickening and heat was assuredly becoming evident to the two pilots. Whatever had started the thermal disturbance in the overhead panels would have been making its presence known in a more alarming fashion.

The type of smoke that develops when plastics and fabrics burn is unlike that of wood or paper. The result is usually a thick, black, soot-laden, noxious substance, which quickly coats any surface it comes in contact with. It infiltrates and chokes, covers, and obscures. In the cockpit of an airplane it can swiftly build to an intensity that lowers light levels, coats instruments on the panels and windscreen, or obscures the pilots' vision, even hanging in the air between them and blinding them to their instruments and the world outside.

Passengers who have survived on-board airliner fires describe scooping the heavy, sooty discharge from their mouth, nose, and eyes, only to have it reassert itself immediately. Without the aid of strong lights and some type of protective covering, the air became so thick with airborne ash that they could not see their hands in front of their face.

Much has been written about the toxic effects of burning plastics and manmade fabrics. They are mostly poisonous and, at best, cause loss of consciousness in confined spaces. Those plastics and metals that yield to the lower melting temperatures will begin to drip, searing hot. If they are driven by some outside agent—such as a burnt-through oxygen line, which could turn the situation explosive, or a breached outer hull that permits the slipstream, driven by 318 knot winds, into the cockpit environment—the flight deck would become a nightmare. The wiring itself needs little encouragement to burn bright and cause proliferate combustion. Kapton arcing occurs at 4,727°C, vapourizing everything in close proximity. At such temperatures there is every reason to suspect that plastics that melt at only 600°C would soon be running out of the overhead, igniting the Mylar drip barrier, and landing on both pilots and the empty jump seat— as later investigations have suggested.

Having just made another fateful turn away from Halifax International, the smoke in the cockpit had probably not yet escalated to the point where the crew was blinded by the ash in the air or were seriously being affected by heat. Something occurred suddenly, though, that made both pilots react and jump immediately to their radios. This could have been due to a sudden outbreak of fire on the flight deck but more likely was a response to total equipment failure. As mentioned, fire extinguishers recovered from the wreckage have indicated that at least three of them were discharged, though investigators have not been able to determine if these were used before the crash or discharged during the impact.

In all the confusion and chaos happening in the cockpit, why did Zimmermann make an apparently deliberate decision to turn to the right? It is every pilot's instinct and training to turn toward the airport, or the next best alternative, when things begin to sour.

Under the circumstances, to turn right seems like a monumental blunder. Though it was the fourth turn, it was the one that would prove fatal. It was likely the only turn not driven by a need to dump fuel, since by now fuel would have been a minor concern. It was possibly the flight crew's last chance—if they were flying blind—to make it into Halifax International Airport. Certainly there was nothing off to their right or to the west that could be of help.

Or was there? True, there are no airports within 100 km of their position. Halifax and Shearwater are closest, with Shearwater being the nearest at only 30 km away and just east of their position. There are no level

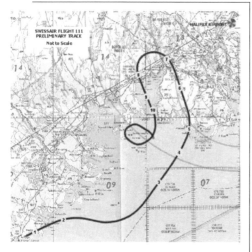

The Flight Track of Swissair 111 as generated by the Transportation Safety Board of Canada. Note number ten is the last communication point with FL-111. The remainder of the track to the impact point is known from radar returns at Halifax International and CFB Greenwood. Below are the altitudes, speeds and the Universal Corrected Times for each of the numbers on the flight track.

1. 1:14:15 UTC HEAD: 086 DEG ALT: 32,900 FT IAS: 291 KTS
2. 1:15:07 UTC HEAD: 102 DEG ALT: 32,900 FT IAS: 292 KTS
3. 1:18:18 UTC HEAD: 054 DEG ALT: 26,500 FT IAS: 302 KTS
4. 1:19:19 UTC HEAD: 049 DEG ALT: 22,800 FT DESC. RATE: -4000 FT/MIN IAS: 311 KTS
5. 1:20:11 UTC HEAD: 026 DEG ALT: 19,800 FT DESC. RATE: -3100 FT/MIN IAS: 320 KTS
6. 1:21:27 UTC HEAD: 360 DEG ALT: 15,700 FT DESC. RATE: -3500 FT/MIN IAS: 318 KTS
7. 1:22:38 UTC HEAD: 335 DEG ALT: 11,900 FT DESC. RATE: -1500 FT/MIN IAS: 319 KTS
8. 1:24:42 UTC HEAD: 179 DEG ALT: 10,200 FT IAS: 318 KTS
9. 1:25:41 UTC END OF FLIGHT RECORDER DATA
10. 1:26:04 UTC LAST SSR RADAR RETURN 9,700 FEET; REMAINDER OF TRACK BASED ON PSR RETURNS (NO ALTITUDE DATA)

areas along that rocky and treacherous coast, or inland, that might have served as a last resort landing place, and even if there were, Zimmermann and Loëw would not have known about them. There is only the flat expanse of the cold, wind-tossed Atlantic or the island-peppered reaches of Mahone Bay—either location an unforgiving landing place for any airplane.

This turn supports my contention that the pilots were heading for a reference to the ground—a lighthouse. As mentioned in chapter eight, I flew over the same track as Flight 111 and was drawn to the lights of Karlson Shipping Company's fish plant at New Harbour Point, and I wondered if the crew of Flight 111 had seen that from the air. If they had lost their instruments, I argued, and had no means to align themselves with the horizontal, then strong ground lights would have given them a necessary reference. But subsequent inquiries about lights I had observed from Grant Kennedy's plane turned up the fact that on the night of our flight, the plant was being used for a movie shoot so the area was well lit with production lighting. Although the plant itself was equipped with powerful lights on the night of September 2 they were not in operation.

Still, there were other lights.

On the southern tip of the Aspotogan Peninsula, due south of the fish processing plant, is an automatic light beacon atop a hill on East Ironbound Island. And seven kilometres southeast of that is another beacon on Flat Island, a tiny near-deserted piece of real estate.

Even though Flight 111 was flying almost directly over Yowler's Light on Paddys Head Island, the flight crew would have lost sight of it under the aircraft's nose, providing they could even see the light through the low cloud layer. Grant Kennedy mentioned seeing Peggys Light at the time he passed through the area; however, he was at an altitude of around 2,000 ft. Zimmermann and Loëw were at a much greater altitude (9,700 ft), and the MD-11's nose would have obliterated a swath of territory at that altitude, including Peggys Light just off to the left and ahead of the nose. It was right over Paddys Head Island that Halifax radar lost Flight 111's Mode C transponder code. Within seconds of losing it, the radar at Halifax and at Greenwood showed Flight 111 turning very gradually to the southwest.

If the MD-11 instrument panel as well as the mechanical, battery-powered backup system had failed, or if air in the cockpit was so thick with smoke that it could not be seen in its low position behind the throttles, a quick glance through the window, only inches away at Loëw's left elbow, might have revealed the automatic light station on East Ironbound Island or its companion on Flat Island. Either lighthouse would have been at a steep downward angle at Loëw's two o'clock but not visible to Zimmermann.

If fire had suddenly broken through into the cabin as I suggested, the sparks or the extreme Kapton arcing could have caused the AI backup battery to fail, would or at least have minimized voltage to below that required to keep the AI's gyro spooled up to a speed (usually around 22,000 rpm) at which it would not tumble. Perhaps whatever caused a massive failure on the instrument panel contributed to a failure of the battery backup. CBs probably begun tripping in a cascade that took out all of the instrument flying aids. Had this not happened then, the pilots would certainly have turned toward Halifax International. Without an AI, however, they could not take the chance. They knew that without a reference to level they would likely get the aircraft into an unusual attitude from which they might not recover. Pilots can lose their sense of reference in as little as five to six seconds or as many as thirty to forty seconds. Once this is lost they really don't have any indication which way is up. So if they saw a light on the ground, which I suspect they did, they would certainly have attempted to use it as their reference to level. Because of the flight path that Flight 111 followed from Paddys Head Island, I believe that they were navigating in reference to the light on either East Ironbound Island, or, and more likely initially, the light on Green Island.

The MD-11's flight path from just a few kilometres southwest of Peggys Cove to East Ironbound is roughly oval in shape, edging in on the west-

Co-pilot Loëw's side of the aircraft. This is actually the nose of the MD 11 that eventually crashed into St. Margarets Bay. It is shown here climbing out of Hong Kong airport.

ern end of the island before swinging back, first to the north and then to the east. In fact the last few kilometres of the flight describe the loop in the backward figure six with East Ironbound situated in the toe of the "six."

If one pilot was busy attempting to quell a fire, or at best keeping it to a bearable level, it left only one pilot to fly the plane. That would leave just one pair of eyes looking out the window, keeping the light in sight, straining to see through goggles that were likely misting over, trying to see through cockpit smoke and attempting to keep the beacon in sight through a thin cloud layer.

If Loëw had spotted the light on the right side of the aircraft, then Zimmermann probably left him to fly the aircraft in relation to it. I believe that Loëw was flying the aircraft for two reasons. First, the lights on East Ironbound Island or Green Island were on his side, the right side of the aircraft, inside the loop of the six and always on the aircraft's right. If things were quickly going wrong on the flight deck, the two pilots would not want to risk a seat change. Furthermore, the cramped quarters with the centre console would have hampered a hasty seat change and could have meant loss of their possible ground reference. The second reason for thinking Loëw was flying is confirmed by the forensic investigation. Loëw's seat restraints were consistent with extreme G-force damage, his DNA was present, and his seat was free of plastic spattering. Captain Zimmermann's seat was clear of spattering as well, which indicates that he was sitting in the seat but not necessarily buckled in. He may have been out of his seat using the fire extinguishers to help drive back the flames or kill the smoke. It's also possible that spattering molten plastics and metals did not actually reach his seat position.

They began to lose altitude—and they would have to lose a great deal to get below the low cloud layer at around 2,000 ft. The fact that they headed for East Ironbound or Green Island light was probably a delaying tactic. They needed a ground reference while they sorted things out.

While the aircraft was rapidly bleeding off altitude—evidenced by the fact that some witnesses saw the aircraft travelling straight and level at or below that low cloud layer—they had to do so without raising their airspeed to dangerous levels. When the aircraft went over Dave Hirtle's house in Blandford, it was not going exceptionally fast. Pilots, of course, know how to lose altitude in each particular aircraft without unduly increasing airspeed. Some of these methods were available to the Flight 111 flight crew, but under the circumstances some were not.

It would have been a risky procedure for the pilots to pull the throttles back to reduce speed because they had no way of knowing their rate of descent or their airspeed. It is necessary to know airspeed to avoid stalling the wings of lift. Maintaining the descent rate is critical to keep the plane from going into an uncontrolled dive rather than allowing it to just bottom out and pancake into the ocean. To lose airspeed and altitude, a pilot can raise the nose of the aircraft without increasing speed. This "aerodynamic braking" uses the aircraft's own body to create drag. But attempting this might have resulted in the loss of forward visibility and, worse still, the loss of their visual reference.

If Loëw were flying at the time, he might have opted for another method, choosing to slip the MD-11 sideways with the nose pointing to the left so as to keep East Ironbound Light on the right side of his windscreen. He could only have accomplished this manoeuvre if he had full control of his ailerons, rudder, and elevators. Since he wouldn't have had the luxury of hearing the engines he was controlling, he would not have been able to decipher what was happening to the plane from their rate of revolutions. At best, without an Air Speed Indicator, Loëw would have reduced the throttles marginally to slow his speed to counter the tendency for the aircraft's speed to increase when making its descent.

The Swissair pilots did have the wing flaps to play with and they were in use, possibly early on when they were making their turns and setting up for their fuel dump. They also had spoilers, a hinged flap that extends upward along the main wing. Spoilers destroy the smooth boundary layer of air that slides over the top of the wing. By deploying the spoilers, the lift created by the smooth airflow over the airfoil causes the aircraft to sink rapidly while maintaining level flight and forward speed. It is uncertain, though, whether these spoilers were in operation during Flight 111's last six minutes.

In a smaller aircraft, pilots can often rely on their own body sensations and sensory input to determine what their airplane is doing—how high it is, how fast it is going, where it is going, and what attitude it has in relation to level. They are close enough to their engines to hear change in pitch and revolutions or slight variations in performance, or to feel subtle changes in attitude. But this is extremely difficult to duplicate in the modern airliner. Seeing out the window is a definite advantage, but the pilots in the modern airliner are so far ahead of the aircraft's centre of gravity and lift (located usually in the vicinity of the main wings) that it is nearly impossible for them to get enough of the an airplane's feel through hydraulic and "fly-by-wire" controls for sensory perceptions to be useful.

In light aircraft, pilots can feel the pressures against the control surfaces right through the control column. They can sense a stall when the aircraft begins a slight buffeting, and shove the nose down to build the airspeed before the whole wing is stalled of its lift. In the large airliner, this sensory input is dampened out by the hydraulics and totally eliminated in fly-by-wire—a system where electrical impulses from the control column are sent to electrical motivators that push or pull the control surface. So engineers have built in artificial stick-shakers to warn the pilots of an impending stall. The trouble is that the warning is generated by a computer, which reads input from detection devices. If the computer fails, as was the case with Flight 111, the pilot's warning devices go right along with it.

We know Zimmermann and Loëw were still dumping fuel because trace amounts were found in small lakes, ponds, and marshes on the tip of the Aspotogan Peninsula several days after the crash. This had to be somewhat detrimental to the aircraft's C of G. In most other aircraft where fuel is located on or near the centre of gravity, (meaning in the wings or an inboard tank close to the C of G) dumping fuel would not greatly affect the C of G. But, as we know, the MD-11 had its third engine on the tail using the rear wings (horizontal stabilizers) to store as much as 6,000 lbs or 3 tons of fuel.

We know No. 2 engine was not running when Flight 111 struck the water, presumably because the fuel pumps were not working due to power loss. In that case, no fuel was being dumped from the rear wing tanks, or being pumped forward to stabilize the aircraft's equilibrium. Though some of the aircraft's fuel was used up in the hour since its takeoff from JFK, the management system would have been replenishing it, pumping it aft from the main wing tanks during the brief flight.

So Loëw had another demon to contend with—a slightly tail heavy aircraft. Trimming the horizontal stabilizers would correct this to a point, but not without power to the tail, which indeed seems to have been the case. Neither the FDR, the CVR, the fuel pumps to No. 2 engine, and not the engine itself—all located in the tail—were working. If the aircraft had become nose high, this would have induced drag, slowing the aircraft down perceptibly, but it would also introduce a loss of lift over the main wings, possibly sneaking the plane into a stall situation. If a sudden loss of reference to the ground occurred, the pilot might inadvertently bank the aircraft one way or the other, or pull up, either action resulting in a loss of lift unless power was applied. If vertigo resulted, the pilot might think that the airplane was in a bank and attempt to bring it back to level, actually maneuvering it into a bank. Lift decreases proportionately to the increased degree of bank angle. As a pilot, I could go on describing the many ways in which loss of lift can occur. Suffice to say that any change from the straight and level decreases lift, due to boundary separation of the air over the wing and to a decrease in speed. Add speed, and a pilot can pull it out, to a point, but even that won't help if the climb angle is too steep.

What we *do* know is that Flight 111 made a sweeping left turn that brought it from a southerly heading on to a westerly track, taking it almost as far out into the Atlantic as Green Island, 6 km (4 mi) southeast of East Ironbound. It, too, has an automatic lighthouse and might have been Loëw's original target. If he lost that light in the low cloud cover, he might have discovered East Ironbound's light only a few kilometres to his northeast. If they were losing altitude rapidly in order to get below the cloud cover at 2,000 ft, they would have been south of East Ironbound Island and its beacon in less than three minutes. Although still uncertain of their altitude they would have known, from the light, they were below the limits of explosive decompression, which can happen if an aircraft doesn't remain sealed, and possibly one or both pilots opened their side windows in an attempt to clear smoke from the cockpit. This could have made matters worse by feeding the fire, and heat would have become a major concern. The fire is guessed to have been behind the bulkhead, about 2 m (6.5 ft) behind the pilots' backs. Molten plastic and aluminum deposits on the jump seat support the theory that fire had travelled forward into the ceiling of the flight deck.

Realizing that they couldn't make the airport, and that time was running out, the pilots had only one option: to ditch the airplane into the Atlantic. No pilot wants to consider ditching a land-equipped aircraft into water. Even in daytime it's a gamble with low odds. At night with no references, the chances are not much better than just crashing the plane. At the landing speeds of the MD-11, water with 1- to 2-m (4- to 6-ft) waves running along its surface is like concrete.

Still, with the heat behind them, smoke surrounding them, and the trackless and impenetrable night before them, the two pilots had only one choice—to crash-land their plane.

The passengers and perhaps most of the flight crew were probably unaware of the battle the pilots were waging in the nose of Flight 111—toxicology tests have indicated that the passengers had not inhaled smoke, strongly suggesting that smoke had not penetrated into the passenger cabin. The plane was flying straight and level, banking gently, and it was likely assumed that there was going to be an annoying delay in their travel schedules from a layover in Halifax. Even the fact that the lights were off (if indeed this was the case; some eye-witness accounts suggest otherwise) would not have caused undue concern, since this is usual during landings anyway.

The MD-11 swept down in a broad banking turn to the right and proceeded northwestward, aiming for a passage that would take it within 1.6 km (1 mi) of East Ironbound Island and 1 km (0.6 mi) north of tiny Flat Island. Its altitude had dropped to about 3,000 ft, and its accumulated descent and forward speed took it by Ironbound Island in a gentle sweeping turn that rocketed the aircraft past the island, almost before the pilots had time to fix its position. Fearful of pulling the throttles back because their real airspeed was unknown to them, they continued the wide looping turn back to the northeast and the tip of the Aspotogan Peninsula.

It's possible that somewhere on the point of the peninsula they spotted a light of some description, or the glow of lights from the small community of Blandford. They continued their turn to the right, passing almost directly over the Hirtle residence in Blandford. Dave Hirtle, alerted by his wife's initial bewilderment over what sounded like tires crunching on their gravel driveway, stepped out on his patio in time to see the belly of Flight 111 emerge from the low cloud layer. The engines were screaming, and he reported the belly was bathed in a yellow light, which suggests that at least a belly beacon might have been still functioning. He watched the MD-11 re-enter the low cloud a few seconds later.

The interior of the same class of plane as Swissair.

Probably unaware of the fact that they were almost out of the low cloud layer, Flight 111 continued further into the Aspotogan Peninsula and just south of Bayswater. Perhaps then they broke through the low cloud and once more obtained the beacon on East Ironbound Island, because the aircraft turned more sharply to the right, almost 90 degrees to its track a moment before. It was once more tracking parallel to the island 4 km (2 mi) away and continuing past it, heading southeast. They maintained this heading for another 7 km (4 mi), about forty seconds, perhaps to regroup, to prepare for the ditching, or perhaps because they were once more distracted by events taking place on the flight deck. Then they made their final turn to the southeast.

This final turn could have been an attempt to keep the light on East Ironbound as a reference. The aircraft was now very low. It must have been extremely difficult keeping the light in sight at the aircraft's considerable speed while attempting to work under the excruciating conditions in the cockpit. The last thing they needed for the hazardous undertaking of ditching on the moody Atlantic was distractions. Despite this final turn, whether or not it was to re-attain the light, Flight 111 was getting further away from East Ironbound Island. The lighthouse there would now have been at Loëw's three o'clock position (the nose being at twelve o'clock), swiftly sliding back to his four-thirty position, a difficult area to see from the window on his right. He was in serious danger of losing sight of the light, and he just might have done so.

If Loëw was flying the airplane, this might have been his moment of truth. This might have been the moment when he realized that he was going to die. He may have looked through the windscreen into a black and featureless void, and suddenly grasped the fruitlessness of his efforts. He simply did not know which way was up. The clouds, the airplane, the lack of detail out on the Atlantic, even those dark seconds between flashes of the lighthouse beacons—just enough time to further confuse his senses—all were conspiring to dash his airplane into the water.

If, in a moment of anxiety, Loëw rolled the MD-11 over in a hard right bank, to recover the light, and it was somehow obscured, he would have experienced vertigo, and lost what tiny link he had with the level state. And where was Zimmermann? Was he incapacitated, perhaps fighting the flames and heat behind them? Or was he, too, sitting at the controls, desperately scanning the black void ahead, looking for any clue as to what their plane was doing?

With reference to the earth's surface lost, the fate of Flight 111 was sealed. While still in a shallow dive, the aircraft began a slow, lateral roll— presumably to its right since that was the general direction just before impact. The roll to the right, was likely the result of overbanking in a right turn. Since the pilots wouldn't have known which way was up, the MD-11 rolled completely over on its back. This roll was probably so gradual that it applied just enough centrifugal force to make the pilots believe, at least briefly, that they were firmly planted in their seats and in an upright position. Once the MD-11 had flipped completely over it might have stabilized for a moment due to inherent stability. But suddenly the pilots would realize they were hanging in their seat belts and that could mean only one thing. They were inverted in their 300-ton airliner.

Except for those trained in aerobatics, a pilot's first instinct when anything goes amiss, is to level the wings, add power, and pull up. And that is likely what they did. The throttles were shoved forward and either one or both pilots hauled back on the control columns. This would have been a grave error. If the plane was inverted instead of climbing, the MD-11 would have begun to describe a downward arc that would take the speed from about 320 knots to well over 600, and possibly beyond Mach one. Investigators estimate that the aircraft hit the water at a speed between 1090 and 1170 kph (600 and 700 mph). This increase in velocity was due to the thrust of Flight 111's own spooling-up jet engines, the natural accelerating effect of pulling around the outside of an arc, and the plane's near vertical attitude aided by it's own weight.

The G-factor would have escalated instantly, from 1 to 6 or 7 Gs, or perhaps even higher. In any event, everyone on board would, mercifully, have greyed out or passed out. Even young, well-trained jet fighter pilots in G suits can't sustain more than 8 or 9 Gs without getting tunnel vision or blacking out. Travelling at a speed of 305 m (1,000 ft) per second, the aircraft would have contacted the surface of the Atlantic less than a couple of seconds after the pilot(s) pulled back on the controls. The water's surface would have been as hard as concrete and less forgiving.

The nose of Flight 111 imploded instantaneously. The sea water rushed upward into the flight deck at, or close to, the speed of sound. The hull held together because it was knife-edging into the water and continued its downward momentum, hitting a ledge at 50 m (55 yd). The tail and the aircraft's mass continued to drive the hull downward, causing the water to rise upward, something like—and just as hard as—the piston in a car engine. It cleared everything in its path, shaving walls clean of their cosmetic covering, ripping wiring free from the harnesses, ramming the bulkheads upwards toward the tail.

The air in the passenger cabin began to compress rapidly, forced upward by the water and contained by the plane's pressure hull, reinforced by the pressure of the water outside the hull and sustained by the aircraft's downward motion. At these speeds, the water was incapable of supporting solubility (dissolving of air into water). The passengers, their seats, and anything else were torn free of their restraints and hurled forward to meet that rising column of water. At about 200 Gs, they were catapulted so violently that when bodies met they literally merged, in some cases into homogeneous masses in which DNA was intermingled.

Several hundredths of a second after the nose of the aircraft slammed into the water, the rising, insoluble mass pressurized the passenger cabin to the point where it exceeded the hull's ability to contain it. The pressure of the sea water still surrounding what was left of the forward end of the aircraft kept it together, channeling the force upward. The 40 percent of the MD-11 that was still out of the water exploded as if a bomb had been planted inside, blasting the plane, luggage, and passengers out over the ocean in thousands of pieces. The rest of the aircraft continued on its destructive path to the bottom, shattering as it went.

In probably less than a second, it was all over. Very likely none of the passengers were even aware of being inverted or of the sudden, violent attempt at a pull-out. They may have been disoriented and confused, perhaps for a moment, but it all happened too quickly for them to have suffered. What remained of Flight 111 was either drifting and tossed on the surface of the ambivalent Atlantic or scattered and buried in the dark depths below.

Who's Next?

My impressions about the safety of airliner travel have changed a great deal since I began this book some nine months ago. During the research it became necessary to look into reasons for other airline crashes to see if there were similarities. There was a common thread to many of them—fire aboard the aircraft that either incapacitated the crew or caused the aircraft's destruction. There was also another thread that developed, related to the first: failure in the miles of wiring in airliners. The crash of Swissair is causing investigators to reconsider past disasters to determine if these crashes—many of them unexplained—were caused by failure in the wiring, leading to a fire that eventually destroyed the machine and took the lives of those on board as it did on Flight 111.

As a pilot I am a proponent of air travel. I love airplanes and flying them. Once it's in your blood, this passion to have hundreds or thousands of feet between yourself and Mother Earth is hard to ignore. To be able to soar and dip and dive, almost as easily as the birds is a heady narcotic, legal, and afforded to relatively few.

Because of my relationship with this aerial environment and the machines that fly through it, it pains me to discover that those who would provide, regulate, and promote this mode of transportation would be less than diligent in their responsibility to keep mass air travel safe. It has become evident to me that both the manufacturers of modern airliners and their owners have allowed the bottom line to rule their thinking. The balance sheet does not only reflect the costs and revenues involved in running an airline; they reflect the number of people who fly in them, and the number who might die. If it happens to be cheaper to pay the insurance claims of a planeload of passengers than to replace faulty equipment, so be it. And it is not only two industries—the manufacturers and the airlines—who demonstrate a lack of concern for the safety of air travellers. In many cases, governments of the countries that produce and/or operate these aircraft are also culpable. There is evidence that even those who are responsible for investigating airline disasters have been less than forthcoming in their conclusions because of political pressures.

Hardly anyone would argue that the reason Swissair Flight 111 crashed was because of a fire caused by faulty wiring. Likely no one would argue that this could have happened in an airplane that had some type of wiring other than Kapton wiring, for possibly the same reasons. What makes Flight 111 unique is that it was known for a good fifteen years before the MD-11 was even *constructed* that Kapton wiring was a ticking time bomb. What is even more frightening is that the aircraft, registered to Swissair in Switzerland, was built six years after the American Navy had stripped Kaptan wiring from some of their military assets, because concerns were so serious. The navy went so far as to permanently ground other military aircraft in their inventory due to the excessive cost of rewiring their planes. Some airlines, specifically American Airlines, had expressed serious reservations about using Kapton wiring in the aircraft about to enter their fleets.

Since this is the case, why did McDonald Douglas allow suspect wiring to be used in the aircraft? And why didn't those regulating the commercial airline industry ensure that Kapton was banned from use?

The crash of Egyptair Flight 990, which apparently was downed by a suicidal pilot in late 1999, is a prime example of why we should do away with the regulation that denies the public's right to know exactly what was said in the cockpit of an airliner shortly before it crashes. The Flight 990 crash has become a political issue. The American NTSB head, James Hall, interfered in the investigation of the crash, casting into doubt the initial findings of his own highly-trained personnel; Egypt refuses to accept that one of their pilots would commit suicide; Egyptair's pilots' association has threatened to sue for defamation anyone who dares to suggest that the pilot intentionally crashed his plane. The association contends that there was an explosion in the tail of the aircraft even though there is no evidence to support this claim. I believe these are reasons enough to allow public access to the CVR tapes. People can then make an informed decision about who they want to fly with.

At the very least, the International Civil Aviation Organization needs to be given the teeth. To hell with a country's competitive position and national pride, an airline's reputation and bottom line, or an association's self-serving protestations. We are talking about the snuffed-out lives of thousands of people and about the millions and millions of air travellers who trust that the industry and its regulating bodies will carry out their responsibility with integrity, without using private or political expediency to cover up facts. There is no place for political maneuvering in airline transportation where safety is concerned. At the time of writing, it appears that, for once, the NTSB in the United States is sticking to its guns, insisting that their best information and their investigations support the contention that the relief pilot on Egyptair 990 aircraft deliberately dove the aircraft into the Atlantic Ocean, killing himself and everyone else aboard, including twenty-two Canadians.

The world's airlines will move billions of people around this planet in the next decade. As we have seen, there is now more to worry about aboard an airliner than the mechanical equipment. There is the wiring, the computers that depend on the wiring, the people who rely on the computers, and the measure of a company's commitment to protect the lives of its passengers and crews. When choosing an airline, the astute passenger should be aware of the airline's commitment to safety rather than the food or the service, or the perks. It would be prudent to choose an airline company that will deal with any potentially dangerous problems and bring them to the attention of the industry and the public so that others might be warned.

Numerous recommendations for change have been made as a result of the Swissair disaster. The CTSB has made specific recommendations to the FAA in the United States, here in Canada, and to other agencies around the world concerning Kapton wiring and Mylar-coated sound and heat insulation, which it now has been discovered helped fuel the fire ignited by the arcing Kapton wire. The CTSB has also made recommendations stipulating that the CVR have a greater duration—at least two hours—rather than the thirty-minute recorders now in place. One would hope that there will also be a stipulation that these recorders be inspected on a frequent basis to insure they are in good working order. There have been cases where the CVRs have survived a crash only to have the investigators discover that the metal tape was balled up inside, useless, and had likely been in that condition for some time. Another recommendation is that CVRs be provided with their own power source; this should include a separate microphone feed in case one is disabled. The FDR has also been targeted, with recommendations that it record up to twenty-four hours before it erases. This is to ensure that possible electronic or mechanical glitches, perhaps from a previous flight, might provide clues to a current disaster. In addition to this are CTSB recommendations that the FDR have its own backup power source.

There is a move afoot to investigate the possibility of having a continuous digital data stream from each aircraft beamed to satellites in geosyncronous orbit around the earth and then transmitted for storage, in case of a disaster. Though expensive, what might make this attractive to the airlines would be the valuable ongoing data they would receive on each flight for maintenance, scheduling, cost of fuel, and much more. This could be a reality within the next ten years.

But let's not fool ourselves. These recommendations are not preventive medicine. If the data stream had been available before Flight 111 crashed, it might have made things easier for the CTSB, but it wouldn't have saved one life. In the case of data stream information in real time, in-flight information might detect something that could alert airline personnel of problems developing somewhere in the aircraft, problems perhaps not readily discernible to the pilots. In a sense this new technology has the promise of predicting troublesome malfunctions before they actually happen, or—if they do happen—of giving the flight crew enough time to react.

My guess, though, is that this will be a reluctant purchase by the airline industry for two reasons: the costs involved and the glitches that will have to be worked out of the systems. Like home security alarms that often go off, causing police to respond to many calls, similar scenarios would probably occur with the new technology, causing a number of unnecessary landings and costly delays for the airlines.

Technology is not the be-all and end-all of the airline industry. It is my contention that the pilots of Swissair Flight 111 lost all available flight instruments, and were reduced to chasing lighthouses off Mahone and St. Margarets Bays to find a reference to the ground. I believe there is a need to get back to basics—for backup purposes at least—and re-instate a few of the older electrically-driven instruments on a "virgin bus" as back-up to the new high-tech systems. The bus should be on its own battery source, generated separately, and not connected in any way to the other electronics in the aircraft. If the main busses failed or something allowed high voltages in low voltage areas (burning them out or destroying the delicate circuits of the on-board computers) then the "virgin bus" would be unaffected and ready to work. Altimeter readings, airspeed and rate-of-climb can be accomplished by using simple barometrics, ambient air pressures, and ram air sources which have more to do with plumbing than with electronics. Many aircraft still use them.

The gyros used in the AI—the instrument that tells the pilots whether the aircraft is level—can be electrically or pneumatically (air) driven. As for finding direction, either a gyroscopically-driven Heading Indicator or a seventy-five-dollar aircraft compass would suffice.

As a pilot, it seems to me that the simplest method (which is often the least expensive) should be used. Venturii/pneumatics driven, gyro-scopically-constructed instruments depend on nothing more than the aircraft's motion through the air in order to run. A venturii—an open metal tube fixed to the outside of the aircraft and aligned with the aircraft's slip-stream (the air moving swiftly along its skin) creates a vacuum in a hollow line, which is hooked into a chamber in the gyro. The vacuum sucks air out of the chamber inside the gyro casing, causing a tiny but powerful jet of air to be drawn into the chamber, which, in turn, strikes a metal fly-wheel with little cups machined into it. The principle is the same as water pouring into the boxes on a waterwheel, causing the flywheel to spin at extremely high rpm, creating a gyroscopic effect. These types of instruments have been around since the 1930s and have been used on airliners for years, not to mention every other type of aircraft flying. The concept is so simple and so cheap that I wonder why the modern airliner doesn't use it for a backup system, rather than rely on battery auxiliary systems.

In this new century, airliners will be travelling at higher altitudes, eventually in sub-orbital flights. This brings with it a retinue of new technical headaches to overcome; unforeseen technical glitches; electrical, mechanical, and structural hazards; even concerns about radiation, which were not an issue in the thick protective envelope of air at Flight Levels 300 and 400. A whole new set of dangers await the passenger in an environment that is instantaneously lethal. A breached hull will not be a matter of just explosive decompression with oxygen masks dropping down in front of the passengers. Oxygen is of no use to a passenger whose blood is boiling due to lack of air pressure at 200,000 ft. At Mach three (3,830 kph or 2,300 mph), or above, a simple structural defect could shred the aircraft. In that environment, would anyone want to fly on an aircraft belonging to an airline whose primary concern was not safety?

If there is any conclusion to be drawn from the tragic end of Flight 111, it is that this disaster could have been prevented. If regulating agencies had exercised their clout and banned Kapton from these aircraft in the mid-1970s, when it was first discovered to be such a volatile material, the aircraft would probably never have crashed. The FAA in the United States had the clout but refused to consider banning Kapton, and still does refuse to consider it a serious hazard to the industry. One might wonder why this government agency would choose to put on blinders in the face of evidence—including the refusal of its own naval air force to use the material. An air force which has grounded those aircraft too expensive to retrofit.

When one explores the back alleys connecting government officials and their individual agendas—their own industries to protect, the jobs that flow from these industries—we always come back to someone's bottom line. Local, state or provincial, and federal politicians; lobbyists; powerful business interests; subcommittees in charge of funding or watchdogging an agency; and the agency itself that answers to the higher power all play a role in determining and upholding that bottom line. If one errs on the side of caution and rules that an airplane shall be grounded or thrown on the scrap heap because the repairs required to avoid a potential problem are just too expensive, and as a result thousands of jobs are lost because a company goes bankrupt, or moves to another jurisdiction then that person's position is in jeopardy because it is the voters who ultimately drive these aircraft. And we all have our bottom lines to worry about, don't we?

Nowadays, almost everyone in economically-developed countries has flown on an airplane. In the last several years the airlines have moved over a billion passengers a year, and that number will expand even more rapidly in the future. Airliners are still the safest way to travel. Nonetheless, people lose their lives—though in very small percentages. The aerospace industry is huge and powerful, but it is still in its infancy. It is a growing and technologically-driven industry. Passengers in this new millennium must come to realize its influence in their daily lives and the freedom of movement it allows. But we need to carefully consider which airliner companies we can trust to carry us safely on business, excursions, or that dream vacation. Be wise and choose carefully. Your life could depend on it.

Related In-flight Aircraft Fires and Accidents

After the highly-publicized 1996 crash of TWA Flight 800 into the Atlantic Ocean off New York City—a crash that killed everyone on board—the media and the public began to take notice of aircraft accidents possibly related to fire as a result of electrical problems. Electrical fires, long known to the Federal Aviation Administration (FAA) in the United States and the Canadian Transportation Safety Board (CTSB), became the focus of worldwide public attention when the crash investigation of Swissair Flight 111 revealed that Kapton wiring was the likely culprit in the cause of the crash. Airliners and airplanes in general do not have to be wired with Kapton for these conduits to be hazardous, or even lethal. Once a fire starts on-board at higher altitudes, where cabin pressures are reduced and the air is thinner, it will probably worsen at lower altitudes, fed by the thicker atmosphere. It is likely that the process of landing could exacerbate the situation.

In the aviation business, there is longstanding knowledge that vibration and the resultant rubbing of one wire against another, against other equipment, or against the metal structures of the aircraft could lead to shorting, popping circuit breakers, or blowing fuses. It is unknown how often this was taken into account by investigators in earlier years when an aircraft suddenly spun out of the sky, though it might be suspected when a subsequent investigation revealed instrument failure or pilot error. The so-called "glass cockpit" of the modern airliner is highly susceptible to wire failure and shorting due to the low voltages used by computers and the related interfacing equipment. High voltages introduced into the sensitive computer environment by a short can wreck havoc. Every airline passenger is familiar with warnings during takeoff and landing about the use of laptop computers and video games. Their possible interference with delicate equipment in the cockpit I personally find rather scary. Simply put, the industry will have to invent ways of keeping the two voltage systems separated.

The following is a list of related airliner incidents and disasters in which wiring seemed to contribute, directly or indirectly, to the accident. It is by no means a complete or representative sampling of the industry, and tends to reflect North American incidents. Some examples are from government agency reports, notably the NTSB (US), the CTSB (Canada), and the Air Accident Investigative Branch (AAIB) in the UK.

On January 9, 1964, an Aerolineas Argentinas Douglas DC-3 took off from Rosario for a scheduled passenger flight to Buenos Aires. Turbulence forced the crew to climb above the flight-plan altitude. The pilot reported a localized fire in the cabin and said he intended to make an emergency landing at Zárate, near Argentina. The aircraft was last seen attempting an emergency landing in a field 9 km (5.4 mi) from Zárate. The plane struck the ground with the undercarriage, left wing, and engine and started to disintegrate. The resultant fire did not consume the entire aircraft, but fatalities included all 3 crew and 25 of the 27 passengers.

Probable cause: "Impact with the ground, for reasons which could not be ascertained, during a precautionary landing. There were fumes or smoke in the cabin and No. 2 engine was cut and its propeller was windmilling, due to oil leakage." [Source: ICAO Aircraft Accident Digest No.16, Circular 82- AN/69 (6-9)]

On September 7, 1964, United Air Lines Vickers Viscount Flight 103 (built in 1955) took off on a scheduled passenger flight from Washington to Knoxville and Huntsville. Near Parrottsville, Tennessee, the aircraft was seen flying at a low altitude, trailing smoke. Whatever occurred on the aircraft was devastating enough to cause a passenger to fall from the plane, followed by a cabin window, possibly the result of a small explosion. The plane then assumed a nose high attitude and lost control. The left wing and nose dropped and the Viscount crashed, killing all 39 people aboard.

Probable cause: "An uncontrollable in-flight fire of undetermined origin, in the fuselage, which resulted in a loss of control of the aircraft." [Source: ICAO Aircraft Accident Digest No.16, Volume III, Circular 82-AN/69 (38-49)]

On September 11, 1968, a fire originated in the rear of the cabin, twenty-one minutes after takeoff. An emergency was declared, but the Air Inter Sud Aviation SE-210 Caravelle jet (built in 1968) crashed into the sea off Nice, France. Fatalities included the 6 crew and all 89 passengers.

Probable cause: While there is little detail on this accident, it is noteworthy that the fire originated in the rear of the aircraft. There are many occurrences of fire in the tail sections of airliners where, coincidentally, there is a great deal of heavy gauge wire supplying voltage to the electric ovens used to heat food. In smaller airliners, washrooms tend to be in the aft section.

July 26, 1969, on a non-scheduled passenger flight to Paris, a Sud Aviation SE-210 Caravelle jet (built in 1961) crashed near Biskra, Algeria, killing 3 of 7 crew and all 30 passengers. A fire reportedly broke out in the electrical compartment and the plane crashed in flames while carrying out an emergency landing.

On July 11, 1973, Varig Airlines Flight 820, originating in Rio de Janeiro, was approaching for landing at Orly International in Paris, France, when the flight crew advised Orly that they had a "problem with fire on board." The crew of the Boeing 707-345C requested an emergency descent. Smoke entered the cockpit and escalated so that pilots had to don oxygen masks and goggles. The smoke grew so thick they could not see their instruments. The captain landed the aircraft 5 km (3 mi) short of the Orly runway. The aircraft landed nose slightly high and banked a bit sheering off trees, tearing off the landing gear and the engines, but the fuselage remained intact. The fire crews from Orly reached the burning aircraft in only six to seven minutes. The flight crew escaped the aircraft along with some of the flight attendants (to a total of 10), but smoke and fumes in the passenger compartment killed all but one of the passengers. (The number of passengers is not available but is suspected to be over 80.)

Probable cause: Investigation led to a cause of either an electrical fault in the right side, aft lavatory, or perhaps careless smoking. Given what we know today, moisture combined with electrical wiring was likely the cause. (Kapton had not been introduced yet into airline construction.)

On November 3, 1973, a Pan American World Airways Boeing 727-321C jet lost control and crashed while on approach at Boston-Logan International Airport. Though not a wiring problem, the cause of the crash was electrical in nature. The aircraft had diverted to Boston because the cockpit was filled with smoke.

Probable cause: "The presence of smoke in the cockpit which was continuously generated and uncontrollable. The smoke led to an emergency situation that culminated in loss of control of the aircraft during final approach, when the crew in uncoordinated action deactivated the yaw damper in conjunction with incompatible positioning of flight spoilers and wing flaps. The NTSB further determines that the dense smoke in the cockpit seriously impaired the flight crew's vision and ability to function effectively during the emergency. Although the source of the smoke could not be established conclusively, the NTSB believes that the spontaneous chemical reaction between leaking acid, improperly packaged and stowed, and the improper sawdust packing surrounding the acid's package initiated the accident sequence. A contributing factor was the general lack of compliance with existing regulations governing the transportation of hazardous materials which resulted from the complexity of the regulations, the industry-wide lack of familiarity with the regulations and the working level, the overlapping jurisdictions, and the inadequacy of government surveillance." [Source: NTSB-AAR-74 -16]

On November 6, 1979, Pakistan International Airlines Flight PK740 (built in 1970) departed on a scheduled passenger flight from Jeddah to Karachi. The Boeing 707 was climbing to 37,000 ft when a flight attendant reported a fire near the aft cabin passenger door. The crew started a descent and were cleared to descend to 4,000 ft. Following a mayday call, nothing more was heard from the flight. The aircraft crashed in a level rocky area at an elevation of 3,000 ft and burst into flames. All 11 crew and 145 passengers were killed.

Probable cause: "An in-flight fire in the cabin area which, through its intensity and rapid extension, resulted in panic among the passengers and smoke in the cockpit, eventually incapacitating the flight crew. The cause of the cabin fire was not determined." It was believed that the origin of the cabin fire could have been a leaking gasoline or kerosene stove, carried aboard by Haj pilgrim passengers. Pressure differential could have caused a poorly sealed gasket to leak fuel. A second possibility is an electrical fire, but the rapid extension of the fire was considered difficult to explain because of the electrical circuit protection devices of the Boeing 707. Sabotage was considered another possibility, but no evidence of use of an incendiary device was found.

On May 27, 1983, a TWA Lockheed L-1011 was descending into Kansas City when a wiring bundle shorted and erupted into flame, causing smoke. The flight engineer used a portable fire extinguisher to put out the fire. The aircraft landed safely in Kansas City.

Probable cause: Investigation cited as cause an electrical wiring short in the windshield anti-ice/de-ice system. The circuit breakers did trip in some instances, but others apparently did not.

On June 2, 1983, Air Canada Flight 797 departed Dallas, Texas, for Montreal via a stopover in Toronto. The aircraft, a DC-9-32, first began to experience difficulties at an altitude of 33,000 ft. The three circuit breakers governing the current to the toilet flush motor tripped. Thinking that the motor might have seized up, the captain waited about eight minutes before attempting to reset the breakers. This proved unsuccessful. The flight attendants reported a strange odour coming from the aft section of the plane and upon investigation discovered that the aft lavatory was full of smoke. A CO2 bottle was used in an attempt to put out the unseen fire. This resulted in thick black smoke issuing from the seams in the lavatory walls. The first officer went back to check and returned to the cockpit to get his goggles. Upon returning to the flight deck, he advised his captain that he thought they should descend. The captain began to experience various electrical difficulties and issued a mayday call, descended, and contacted Cincinnati. Smoke began to fill the passenger compartment. He made an emergency landing at Cincinnati, where the aircraft began to burn rapidly. Though many escaped the burning aircraft, others died before they could evacuate.

Probable cause: Originally, the motor was believed to be the cause of the fire. It is now believed that the more likely causes were the Kapton wiring supplying voltage to the motor and moisture dripping on the wire—a lethal combination where Kapton is concerned—along with the pilot's repeated attempts to recycle the circuit breakers. It has been discovered on subsequent occasions that this recipe for disaster has contributed to lavatory fires in DC-9s and other types of aircraft.

On June 25, 1983, a few weeks after the Air Canada incident, another McDonnell Douglas DC-9-51 experienced a near-identical calamity. An Eastern Airlines flight that had just touched down in Tampa, Florida was taxing in from the landing when it had a fire in its aft lavatory, which began under the toilet seat. Attempts to contain the fire were unsuccessful, resulting in substantial peripheral damage to the area surrounding the lavatory. In this case, however, the 77 passengers and crew were able to evacuate without injuries.

Probable cause: The cause of the fire was undetermined. However, one could speculate that either the toilet motor or the wire supplying voltage might have been the culprit because this was the same type of motor and the same wiring which destroyed Air Canada flight 797 a few weeks before.

On October 7, 1983, while taking off from Juneau, Alaska, a Western Airlines Boeing 727-247 developed smoke in the cockpit, which dissipated then reappeared. The aircraft landed safely. None of the 87 passengers and crew were injured.

Probable cause: Investigation revealed that a switch controlling voltage to the right-hand taxi light had overheated and failed, burning up in the process. During the course of this failure, it also burned through the insulation of a wire in a wire harness next to it. The Boeing 727 was wired with Kapton. Note: This was the third incident involving wire-related smoke or equipment failure caused by wire in the space of six months.

On May 17, 1984, a McDonnell Douglas DC-10-4, carrying 239 passengers and crew, was climbing out of 33,000 ft for 37,000 ft when the first officer saw sparks, then smoke, coming out of the panel in front of him, just below the glare shield. The cockpit lights were extinguished manually and the smoke stopped. The captain aborted the flight and landed back in Minneapolis, Minnesota, without further mishap.

Probable cause: The investigation revealed a wiring bundle—re-installed only four days before—that had been stretched across a florescent light bracket and forced to turn an abrupt angle around its sharp edge. The sleeve around the wires and the insulation was burned, leaving the metal wire core bare, probably as a result of vibration, causing the sharp metal edge to wear through the protective insulation. It shorted out; however, the circuit breakers did not function as they should. Quick response by the pilots in isolating the circuits by manually shutting off power to them likely averted a more serious situation. The investigators were unable to determine why the circuit breakers did not pop. They listed the cause as chafed electrical wiring and electric wire arcing. The DC-10 Kapton was introduced into aircraft production in 1976, eight years earlier. This is an indication as to how far back some of these incidents may go.

On May 17, 1984, a Republic Airlines, Inc. Boeing 727 on a scheduled 14 CFR 121 operation levelled at Flight Level 330, when the No. 2 engine fire warning light and bell activated. The crew followed the published procedures, shut down the engine and used a fire bottle (a device similar to a fire extinguisher that is mounted on or near the engine to douse a fire). They then diverted to Cincinnati and made a precautionary landing. After landing, fire department personnel reported to ground control a "small amount" of smoke from the No.1 engine. In turn, ground control relayed this information to the crew, without the words "small amount," as the plane was taxiing. The aircraft was stopped and evacuated using the escape slides. One passenger was seriously injured when a slide burst. There was evidence it was punctured by a shoe nail after the shoe heel came off.

Probable cause: Investigation revealed there was a false fire warning indication due to a shorted fire detector.

On May 30, 1984, the four-man crew of a Lockheed L-188 were at 22,000 ft over Pennsylvania when things suddenly began to go wrong. (Most of what is known about the incident comes from the CVR.) Due to a fault in the No. 2 Vertical Gyro System (VGS), the captain selected the No. 1 VGS. Shortly after there were indications of confusion in the cockpit, apparently to do with maintaining level flight. Only seconds later the aircraft went into a right descending spiral dive. The airspeed rose rapidly and the aircraft broke up in flight. Wreckage was found over an area 3 km (2 mi) long by about 2 km (1 mi) wide. The crew was killed.

Probable cause: The NTSB listed, as a contributing factor, the lighting conditions during the flight, "a dark night." For some reason AIs, the primary flight instruments for maintaining level flight, failed. They are electrically driven in this aircraft. There was no back-up AI. Without these, the flight crew was doomed.

On December 4, 1984, a Northwest Airlines Boeing 727-251, while in cruise operation, reported that an electrical fire had erupted in the circuit board and in electrical components of the temperature control unit for the rear galley oven. The associated circuit breaker was opened, electrical power to the galley was turned off, and within minutes the unit was cool to touch. The flight crew opted to land the aircraft at Atlanta, Georgia, as a precaution. All 99 people aboard were uninjured. The manufacturer of the unit is reportedly no longer in business. Fortunately, the overheated oven temperature control circuitry was enclosed in metal box. Northwest Airlines has reported that this type of failure has been a chronic problem. On December 7, 1984, the company began to retrofit remaining units with a circuit modification.

Probable cause: An electrical system and an electric wiring failure. Over temperature in an electrical temperature control box. Note: In this case the circuit breaker supposedly protecting the wiring to this component did not activate on its own. The problem circuitry had to be isolated manually. It's a fact that sometimes circuit breakers don't work. [Source: NTSB Identification: ATL85IA047]

On May 11, 1990, a Philippine Air Lines Boeing 737-3Y0 exploded while being pushed back by ground handlers prior to flight in Manila. The centre fuel tank exploded, reminiscent of the explosion aboard TWA Flight 800, pushing the floor of the aircraft upwards. The outboard tanks caught fire and the aircraft was completely destroyed.

Probable cause: Investigation found no evidence of a bomb, incendiary device, or detonator. The centre tank contained only fumes and a few gallons of fuel. Possibly, like TWA 800, an electrical fault initiated the blast.

On November 24, 1993, a Scandinavian Airlines System McDonnell Douglas MD-87 was taxiing to the gate for takeoff on a scheduled passenger flight from Copenhagen, Denmark. A flight attendant smelled smoke, which continued to develop, and all 85 people on board were safely evacuated at the gate. A fire substantially damaged the fuselage skin and destroyed the aft interior of the plane.

Probable cause: Investigation found the origin of the fire in two electrical wires that provided 115-volt alternating current (AC) to a utility plug in the right stowage closet, and 28-volt AC to lights in the stowage closet and the emergency drawer at the bottom of the closet, respectively. The wires were found to be slack between two supports and became pinched because they were not adequately secured.

On June 25, 1996, shortly after a Delta Air Lines Boeing 767-332ER departed from Jamaica, New York, the flight crew heard a loud pop or crack, and the airplane made an uncommanded roll to the left. In addition, the right generator Off light illuminated. By holding continuous input to the control yoke, the flight crew regained a wings-level attitude and returned for an overweight landing without incident. The 229 people on board were uninjured.

Probable cause: The improper installation of the generator feed cable by the manufacturer, which resulted in a severed aileron cable due to arcing between the generator feed cable and aileron cable. Examination of the airplane revealed that one of two aileron cables on the right side aileron control had been severed by electrical arcing from the right engine generator feed line. No evidence of contact between the generator feed cable and the aileron cable was found. However, a pinhole about 1/8 in. in diameter was found on the plastic sheath of the generator feed cable near the area where the aileron cable passed. According to the Boeing drawing used for production, a 1 in. minimum clearance between the aileron cable and the generator feed line should be maintained. When the aileron cable was replaced and tensioned on the incident airplane, clearance between the aileron cable and generator feed line was measured at 3/16 in.

On July 17, 1996, TWA Flight 800, a Boeing 747 out of JFK Airport, New York, heading for Paris, France, was climbing through 13,800 ft to its assigned altitude. Twelve minutes into the flight, communications were suddenly lost and shortly after the plane was lost from radar. Eye-witnesses, many of them airline pilots in the vicinity, reported an explosion in TWA 800's location. The nose section of the Boeing 747 separated from the aircraft and began tumbling to the Atlantic Ocean below. The remainder of the aircraft rotated sharply upward and, with its four engines still developing full thrust, continued to climb another 2,000 ft before it entered a high-speed wing-stall state, rolled over, and went into a dive. The airspeed reached a point that exceeded the design limitations of the aircraft, and the wings were torn off. Thousands of gallons of fuel from the wings ignited and entered the passenger compartment as the plane continued its fiery plunge into the Atlantic, killing all 230 people aboard.

Probable cause: After more than a year of debris recovery from the floor of the Atlantic, and of intensive, often controversial, investigation, it was officially determined that the centre fuel tank—a massive reservoir located just behind the cockpit and the first-class passenger compartment and lounge—exploded. At the time, the tank was empty of fuel but full of fumes. Though to date the NTSB has been unable to locate the trigger, it is believed that a thin sensor wire (using only tiny voltages) passing through the tank shorted out or came in contact with another high voltage wire, which caused a flash in the tank and the subsequent explosion.

On September 5, 1996, flight crew determined there was smoke in the cabin cargo compartment on a Federal Express Corporation McDonnell Douglas DC-10-10CF. The pilots declared an emergency and the flight was diverted to Newburgh/Stewart International Airport, New York. After a safe landing, the airplane was destroyed by fire. Three people aboard were uninjured, and 2 received minor injuries. The fire burned for about four hours after smoke was first detected.

Probable cause: An in-flight cargo fire of undetermined origin. Investigation revealed that the deepest and most severe heat and fire damage occurred in and around container 6R, which contained a DNA synthesizer holding flammable liquids. However, there was insufficient evidence to conclude where the fire originated. The flammable chemicals in the DNA synthesizer was unintended and unknown to the preparer of the package and shipper. The captain did not adequately manage his crew resources. He failed to call for checklists and to monitor the accomplishment of required checklist items. Note: More recent information on chafing wires suggest that this fire may have started electrically and possibly under the floor then spread into the cargo container, rather than the other way around.

On February 20, 1997, Northwest Airlines McDonnell Douglas DC-9-15 Flight 219 experienced an in-flight electrical fire, which filled the cockpit with smoke and fumes. The crew on this scheduled passenger flight donned their oxygen masks and turned off both generators and the battery switch. They flew with a flashlight for one minute, then turned the emergency power switch on after the flames had extinguished themselves. They declared an emergency and landed at Des Moines, Iowa. None of the 36 occupants were injured.

Probable cause: The electrical fire originated within the power distribution systems cross-tie relay, due to a short circuit.

On January 9, 1998, a United Airlines Boeing 767 Flight 967, en route to Washington from Zurich, experienced electrical difficulties and aborted its overseas flight to land at Heathrow in London. The flight crew began to experience unrelated electrical difficulties northwest of Paris. Upon landing at Heathrow, the flight attendants reported smoke in the first-class passenger cabin. The passengers were quickly evacuated, with some minor injuries.

Probable cause: The AAIB noted ten popped circuit breakers on the flight deck and discovered Kapton arc tracking in a wiring bundle next to a refrigeration unit, called a chiller, which resulted in damage to other wiring in the bundle. There was clear evidence of arc tracking with the presence of molten beads of copper and a burned section of insulation in the wiring harness. The AAIB investigative team, along with the American NTSB, attempted to discover if the first-class galley's chiller unit wiring harness may have been damaged during previous maintenance, and whether the maintenance people may have nicked insulation on a wire in the damaged bundle while removing it from the equipment bay. The AAIB also noted that the Kapton wiring was mixed in with another type of wiring and insulation, which is not common practice and is frowned upon by FAA regulations.

On December 15,1998, Delta Air Lines Boeing 737-232 Flight 2461, registered to Wilmington Trust Company Trustee, reported a total loss of electrical power on a scheduled domestic passenger/cargo flight as gear and flaps were extended on approach for landing at Orlando International Airport, Florida. Visual meteorological conditions prevailed and an IFR flight plan was filed. The airplane sustained minor damage. The airline transport-rated pilot-in-command (PIC), first officer (FO), 3 flight attendants, and 51 passengers reported no injuries.

The FO was flying the airplane. All descent and approach checklists were completed. The Auxiliary Power Unit (APU) was started on base leg. The FO called for the gear and flaps 15. The airplane experienced a total loss of electrical power The APU did not start, and the battery indicated between 17 and 18 volts (out of 24). The normal checklist procedures were accomplished followed by the quick reference procedures. The flight crew were unable to restore electrical power. A go-around was initiated to continue the checklist. All communications and electrical equipment failed. The flap indicator showed an asymmetrical setting. A flight controllability check was accomplished with no anomalies. The flight continued and the plane was landed. A left main landing gear tire blew out on rollout. The airplane cleared the runway, stopped, and was towed to the ramp.

Probable cause: A detailed inspection of the aircraft's electrical system was made, which required the removal of numerous electrical system components for further tear-down inspections, including an operational check of all related cockpit systems and a flight test following all on-board troubleshooting and component replacements. The problem components were sent to Delta's maintenance facility in Atlanta, Georgia, for a preliminary inspection then sent on to Boeing Aircraft Company in Seattle, Washington for further testing.

On June 22, 1999, United Air Lines Boeing B-737-300 Flight 281 en route from Minneapolis, Minnesota, to Denver, Colorado, reported smoke and "electrical smell" in the cabin. The captain diverted the flight to Scottsbluff, New England, the nearest approved alternate. The flight crew turned off all non-essential equipment and landed. There were no injuries among the 63 people aboard, and the airplane was not damaged.

Probable cause: The exact source of the smoke was not found, there were no "hot spots" in the cabin, and there was no indication of a lightning strike. The airplane was tested and ferried to Denver for further examination. The irregularities did not recur during the flight.

On September 17, 1999, a Delta Air Lines McDonnell Douglas MD-88 Flight 2030, made a precautionary landing at the Cincinnati/Northern Kentucky International Airport (CVG), Covington, Kentucky. There were no injuries to the 5 crew and 113 passengers. The airplane received minor damage. Flight 2030, on a scheduled 14 CFR 121 operation, was following an IFR flight plan. As the airplane was climbing through Flight Level 230 (23,000 ft), the flight crew reported smoke in the cabin and declared an emergency. The airplane was handed off to Covington Approach Control for return to CVG. The airplane landed and was stopped on the runway. Emergency exits were activated, and occupants exited the airplane.

Probable cause: Initial examination of the airplane revealed thermal damage under the main cabin floor and behind the aft side of the forward cargo door on the right side of the fuselage—the same area where the right side alternate static port is located. The damage consisted of sooting and heat distress to the underside floor structure and to a fiberglass portable water bottle. The covering on three metalized Mylar insulation blankets was missing and the edges of the blankets were charred. A fiberglass cargo bin wall panel in the vicinity was burned. Also, soot damage was visible in the cabin on the right side wall in the vicinity of passenger row eleven. The heating element for the primary and alternate static sources, controlled from a cockpit switch, could be activated on the ground or in the air. A thermal sensor regulates the temperature of heating elements within predetermined limits. The circuit breaker to the electric heat for the static ports, located in the cockpit, had not tripped. An insulation resistance check made on the right side alternate static port heater revealed lower-than normal-resistance. The heater element plate and associated hardware were retained for further examination.

On January 31, 1999, American Airlines McDonnell Douglas MD-11 Flight 27 made an emergency landing at the Seattle-Tacoma International Airport due to smoke in the cabin. The 16 crew and 64 passengers were not injured. The 14 CFR Part 121 scheduled international passenger flight had departed Seattle en route to Narita, Japan. According to representatives of American Airlines, the airplane was airborne for about one hour ten minutes while cruising over north Vancouver Island, British Columbia, when the event occurred. A "buzz" was first heard over the public address system, so the flight crew reset the circuit breaker for it. Smoke was then observed in the first-class cabin area. The crew immediately declared an emergency and turned back to Seattle. A crew member located the source of the smoke and opened up an overhead bin just forward of the R2 door, located near the right rear section of the first-class cabin. A halon fire extinguisher was discharged onto a video system control unit (VSCU) and the smoke dissipated without further incident. No reports of fire were made.

Probable cause: No fire damage was found. Examination of the VSCU by the FAA revealed that part of a circuit board was charred. Further examination of the entire video system revealed internal damage to several video distribution units (VDUs) downstream of the VSCU. A "cannon plug" power connector that linked the damaged components showed evidence of moisture damage and a short circuit between two pins. All video system wiring was intact and undamaged. The video system was manufactured by Rockwell Collins Passenger Systems and certified by the FAA Long Beach Aircraft Certification Office. It was installed in the incident airplane by McDonnell Douglas prior to the aircraft's delivery from the factory. According to manufacturer records from Rockwell Collins, the connector failure was the first of its kind. This NSTB report contains preliminary information and is, therefore, incomplete.

Glossary

AI — Attitude Indicator,* also known as ADI (Attitude Director Indicator). This instrument shows a representation of the sky above and the ground below. It is a gyroscopically-driven precision instrument used to indicate to the pilot whether the airplane is nose high or low, and whether the wings are parallel to the ground. The pilot can tell if the airplane is climbing or banking or a combination of the two.

Ailerons — The hinged control surfaces at the trailing edge of the wing tips. When deflected they operate in opposite directions on each wing tip. This causes the airplane to bank. One deflects upward while the other deflects downward. The upward deflecting surface kills lift, causing the wing to drop, while the other causes a greater curving or camber to the opposite wing, which creates more lift, causing that wing to lift.

ATC — Air Traffic Control

APU — Auxiliary Power Unit. A small jet, usually in the rear of the aircraft, with a generator that supplies ground power to the airliner for instruments, lighting, air conditioning, and start-up power for the main engines.

CAF — Canadian Armed Forces

CFB — Canadian Forces Base

CRT — Cathode Ray Tube. Essentially a TV screen, used extensively now for the main screen displays on the instrument panel. The newer models are flat screen LCDs (Liquid Crystal Displays).

CTSB — Canadian Transportation Safety Board

EFIS — Electronic Flight Instrument System. This term includes just about every instrument in the cockpit of the modern airliner.

Elevators — The flaplike appendages on the horizontal tail surfaces (horizontal stabilizers) of an airplane. They are used to cause the nose of the airplane to pitch up or down, depending on their deflection.

EMO — Emergency Measures Organization

FAA — Federal Aviation Administration

FADEC — Full Engine Digital Control Authority

Flaps — A portion of the inboard section of the trailing edge of the wing, which slides backward and down to create high lift at low speeds while maintaining stable flight characteristics. On airliners they are usually hydraulically actuated. Used primarily for takeoff and landings.

FMS — Flight Management Systems

FPM — feet per minute

HI — Heading Indicator* This gyroscopically-driven instrument displays the face of the compass with a pointer indicating the direction the airplane is flying. The pilot has to set the HI by looking at his real compass to see which bearing (in degrees) it is indicating; he then turns a knob that brings up the proper bearing under the pointer on the face of the HI dial.

HIA — Halifax International Airport.

HSI — Horizontal Situation Indicator, also HI.* This instrument displays the face of the compass on it, marked off in degrees, with a pointer indicating the direction the airplane is flying. The HSI is also a gyroscopically-driven instrument; it is maintained in memory and needs no setting.

I/C — Intercom. Allows the pilots to communicate via headsets in a noisy environment.

ICAO — International Civil Aviation Organization. A governing body that makes the rules concerning civil aviation.

IFR — Instrument Flight Rules. Required for flying "blind" or flying without visual reference to the ground. It's used by any pilot that has this endorsement on his flying licence. To obtain an IFR ticket takes many hours, a great deal of training with "flying on instruments," and a lot of money. Any pilot with the requisite number of hours and ratings can take training to get an IFR endorsement on their pilot's licence. All airline pilots flying passengers have a multi-engine IFR rating.

ILS — Instrument Landing System. Used at airports set up for ILS to make instrument approaches at night and during bad weather.

Knots — Nautical miles per hour. Add 15 percent to get mph; 100 knots is about 192 kph (115 mph).

Mach — The speed of sound. At sea level where the air is thick, Mach one is about 1,113 kph (668 mph); at 30,000 ft, about 1.293 kph (776 mph).
Moncton Centre
That sector of the air navigation and control of airspace from 12,500 ft upward that controls aircraft at flight levels and corridors through their sector.

NTSB — National Transportation Safety Board

PTT — Push To Talk switch. A button on the control yoke of the aircraft that the pilot or co-pilot pushes when transmitting a radio message.

QAR — Quick Access Recorder. A lightweight maintenance recorder usually housed on the flight deck or in the equipment bay. It records certain aircraft functions such as hydraulics, or data, for the edification of the maintenance crews.

RCC — Rescue Coordination Centre. A function of the military (CAF) with a link to the Canadian Coast Guard. It's usually the primary contact for anyone reporting either a missing airplane or vessel. The RCC assigns the proper authority—Coast Guard, RCMP, naval, air, or troop assets—to whatever search and rescue requirements are indicated.

Rotate — Rotation. The point at which the pilot determines that the aircraft's speed, while still on the runway, is sufficiently above the aircraft's (wing) stalling speed and ready to fly. The pilot pulls back on the controls, lifting the nose wheel off the runway in preparation to fly.

ROV — Remotely Operated Vehicle. A submersible, unmanned vehicle used to locate and retrieve material from the deep ocean. They are equipped with electric motors, a video camera, lights, and sometimes grappling devices. Tethered by a long umbilical cord to another manned submersible or to a surface ship, they serve as eyes and as an alternate recovery vehicle to human divers in situations too hazardous to risk the human counterpart.

Runway Headings — These are in degrees magnetic to the nearest 5 degrees and always in tens all the way around the compass from 10 to 360; however, the last digit is dropped. For example Runway 10 is denoted as 010 but the last digit is dropped, meaning it is painted on the runway as 01. A runway heading dead north magnetic would be at 360 degrees but is painted on the runway as 36. The other end of the runway is the reciprocal of 360; 180 degrees away being runway 18. East-west runways are more common in the east since the wind is frequently out of the west. So runways 27-09 and 28-10 are often seen on the charts. These are just examples.

SAR — Search and Rescue

SARtech — Search and Rescue Technician. Highly trained military personnel for air, sea, and land operations.

Slats — A portion of the leading edge of the wings that slides forward and droops to enhance the high lift/slow speed capability of the extended flaps at the trailing edge of the wings.

Stall or stalling — In the flying business, stall or stalling does not refer to the engine's performance or its lack thereof but to the ability of the mainplanes (wings) to sustain lift. When they do not have sufficient air travelling over them or when the angle at which wing meets air is too great, the wing will cease to generate lift and is said to stall.

T&B — Turn and Bank Indicator

TCU — Terminal Control Unit

Tower — The tower in a controlled airspace is usually responsible for local traffic that has entered its zone. At Halifax International Airport the zone extends out from the tower 7 nautical miles, with the top of its zone at 3,500 ft To enter the zone you must get permission and have certain equipment.

Transponder — This device, located on the instrument panel in the radio rack, senses a radar pulse and, within microseconds, amplifies this pulse and sends it back with the aircraft's radar reflection, thereby making the target on the controller's screen much brighter and larger. The transponder also sends a code also , which is set by the pilots in the cockpit. When ATC wants to insure a plane's position and identity, they ask the pilot to "squawk ident." The pilot presses a button on the transponder that further enhances the radar return. If ATC wishes to remain with that target they give the pilot a new code (which the pilot dials in and re-squawks) to maintain that aircraft's identity on the scope. The code also sends the aircraft's altitude if it is "Mode C" equipped, which all airliners are. In this manner ATC maintains aircraft separation.

TSB — Transportation Safety Board

VFR — Visual Flight Rules. The method of piloting an airplane that requires flying with reference to outside details such as the horizon, lights, or any ground reference, but within certain limitations; these are restrictions on flying with a ceiling or solid cloud cover with a low ceiling. Every pilot starts out this way before moving on to any other endorsement.

VSI/ROC — Vertical Speed Indicator or Rate-of-Climb.* The VSI indicates to the pilot the number of feet per minute that the airplane is climbing or descending. Rate-of-climb indicates the same in knots.

* *On the modern airliner, most of these instruments are shown as an animation on the flat screen display in front of the pilot. It looks like the face of the real instrument but is only a read-out from the real instrument, which is buried in the equipment bay. Its electrical signal is transmitted through wiring to the flat screen display.*

CONVERSION TABLES   used to calculate
knots, miles per hour, and kilometres per hour:

knots x 1.15 = mph (for example, 100 knots = 115 mph)
knots x 1.92 = kph (for example, 100 knots = 192 kph)
kph x .6 = miles per hour (for example, 100 kph = 60 mph)